GANGS, GUNS
AND KNIVES

by the same author

We Need to Talk about Pornography
A Resource to Educate Young People about the Potential
Impact of Pornography and Sexualised Images on
Relationships, Body Image and Self-Esteem
ISBN 978 1 84905 620 5
eISBN 978 1 78450 091 7

101 Things to Do on the Street
Games and Resources for Detached, Outreach and
Street-Based Youth Work, Second Edition
ISBN 978 1 84905 187 3
eISBN 978 0 85700 419 2

Working with Young Men
Activities for Exploring Personal, Social and
Emotional Issues, Second Edition
ISBN 978 1 84905 101 9
eISBN 978 0 85700 282 2

Working with Young Women
Activities for Exploring Personal, Social and
Emotional Issues, Second Edition
ISBN 978 1 84905 095 1
eISBN 978 0 85700 372 0

GANGS, GUNS AND KNIVES

Activities and Lesson Plans to Raise Awareness
with Young People Aged 14–19 about the
Risks and Realities of Gang-Related Crime

Vanessa Rogers

Jessica Kingsley Publishers
London and Philadelphia

First published in Great Britain in 2021 by Jessica Kingsley Publishers
An Hachette Company

1

Copyright © Vanessa Rogers 2021

Front cover image source: Shutterstock®.

A CIP catalogue record for this title is available from the
British Library and the Library of Congress

ISBN 978 1 78775 088 3
eISBN 978 1 78775 089 0

Printed and bound in Great Britain by TJ Books Ltd

Jessica Kingsley Publishers' policy is to use papers that are natural, renewable and recyclable products and made from wood grown in sustainable forests. The logging and manufacturing processes are expected to conform to the environmental regulations of the country of origin.

Jessica Kingsley Publishers
Carmelite House
50 Victoria Embankment
London EC4Y 0DZ

www.jkp.com

Contents

Section Three: Decision-making

Section Four: Staying safe

About the Author

Vanessa Rogers is a qualified teacher and youth worker and is an experienced manager of services for children and young people, including youth work, social care and the preventative wing of a youth offending team. She is commissioned across England, Scotland, Wales, Ireland and the Channel Islands as a freelance trainer, offering a wide range of courses to youth services, schools, social care and voluntary sector professionals working with 13- to 19-year-olds (up to 25 with additional needs), especially those identified as at risk/vulnerable. Her interactive and lively workshops and webinars include online safety and social media; gangs, guns and knives; work with young women; body image and emotional wellbeing; LGBTQ+ support; and drug and alcohol awareness. Professional development courses including safeguarding, adolescent development and managing challenging behaviour are also available.

Vanessa also designs and delivers workshops directly to young people, for example training volunteer Youth Health Champions (Hertfordshire), training peer mentors to provide sexual health support and delivering safeguarding workshops to social work apprentices.

As well as designing and delivering her own workshops, Vanessa Rogers is an Associate Trainer/Consultant for several well-respected youth organizations including UK Youth, the National Youth Agency and KIP Education. This includes writing content for online courses, delivering webinars, designing bespoke training, contributing to local and national programmes in health, youth offending, education and the voluntary sector, and developing courses accredited through NVQ, OCN and City & Guilds. She is also a guest contributor for the podcast 'The Sex Ed Diaries', a series focusing on the changes to Relationships and Sex Education (RSE) in English schools, hosted by Dr Polly Haste, in partnership with sexual health and wellbeing charity, Brook. She sits on the council for The Institute for Youth Work, which is a membership organization for Youth Workers and those that espouse youth work methodologies and ethics in their work with young people.

Feedback and testimonials can be found at www.vanessarogers.co.uk.

In addition to training Vanessa is commissioned to undertake peer reviews, evaluations and community consultations. These include an evaluation of youth work in schools for the Welsh Government, a Big Lottery Fund three-year external evaluation of a young parents project in South Wales, a peer review of children's services in the London Borough of Islington and a community consultation in Somerset. She is experienced in developing peer education and mentoring projects, developing joint agency detached and outreach projects and setting up youth governance structures that enable young people to have their say on local issues.

Vanessa maintains her professional practice through short-term contracts in Children and Young People's Services both as a manager and practitioner. Most recent contracts were for Hertfordshire County Council and Peterborough Borough Council where she was tasked with developing targeted support and preventative projects for vulnerable children and young people most at risk of grooming for criminal and sexual exploitation, in particular those associated with gangs and county lines. Other work includes developing projects for LGBTQ+ and trans young people and their families, setting up multi-agency projects to reduce the risk of trafficking, developing a network of parenting groups (both voluntary and for those on parenting orders), anger management programmes and workshops for the victims and perpetrators of domestic abuse and stalking.

Preface

Whilst gangs and gang-related crime continue to be part of the national conversation, and hard-hitting headlines report a rise in street violence and child homicides, it's important to remember that the vast majority of young people in the UK are not involved with gangs, guns and knives, and probably never will be.

Meeting friends in a public space is not a crime, and being part of a friendship group is a normal part of growing up for the majority of young people. It's important that the differences between this and street-based gangs with crime and violence at their core are clarified so that all young people are not demonized and that those most vulnerable to coercion and control can be protected.

> Victims and offenders are often the same people. When adults treat a young person as just a victim or just an offender, they are not taking into account the complex, cyclical nature of the victim–offender link and the factors that influence young people's lives.[1]

This, and the gap between actual crime and the perceptions of crime are explored within this book, along with the reasons why someone might join a gang and what they potentially get out of it, both positive and negative.

Activities to explore gangs, gang-related crime and anti-social behaviour can be used as standalone interventions or as linked activities that build together to reinforce key messages, supporting young people to develop the skills and attitudes to make healthy choices and stay safe. They challenge common gangster stereotypes of money, power and fame seen in films, music videos and social media, and the mistaken belief that carrying a weapon 'protects you', to raise awareness about the emotional and physical risks of gang life as well as the legal consequences of violent crime, which can include life imprisonment.

> …it is important not to 'over dramatise' the carrying of knives. It can be easy to inadvertently 'glamorise' the carrying of knives. Instead teaching should focus on helping young people to develop the understanding needed to recognise when a situation is becoming dangerous, the language and skills required to stay safe, an understanding of the law and an appreciation of the full extent of the consequences of a knife crime.[2]

Finally, young people are encouraged to consider the wider impact that gangs and violence has, not just on those perpetrating it, but also on their family, friends and the wider community.

---

1   Owen, R. and Sweeting, A. (2007) *Hoodie or Goodie? The Link between Violent Victimisation and Offending in Young People: A Research Report.* London: Victim Support.
2   Taken from the website of The Ben Kinsella Trust, www.benkinsella.org.uk

Introduction

This book provides a toolkit of resources for youth workers, teachers, social workers and youth justice practitioners to raise awareness with young people aged 14–19 about the risks and realities of gangs and gang-related violent crime. All references to 'children' or 'young people' mean those under the age of 18, as defined in the Children Acts 1989 and 2004.[1] Whilst not specifically aimed at those already immersed in gang life or known to the criminal justice system, activities can be adapted to meet specific needs to help reduce the risk of re-offending.

Divided into four sections of activities, each activity offers a different learning experience enabling facilitators to deliver standalone sessions on a single issue or mix and match different topics to form a robust curriculum that builds on learning over time.

Section One provides an understanding of what a gang is and the differences between gangs and friendship groups, and explores why some young people are attracted to gang life. In addition it enables young people to separate out some of the myths about gangs from the facts.

Section Two explores attitudes to risk taking and considers how personal values and attitudes to crime can shape decisions made. It also looks at the short- and long-term risks of law breaking, and offers information about the criminal justice system to enable young people to make informed decisions.

Section Three moves on to consider the role of peers and peer pressure in gang life. It explores the relationships that can influence decision-making, and encourages young people to stop and consider the potential consequence of actions, as well as providing strategies for being assertive. Finally, it offers some positive role model activities to inspire and motivate young people and help them realize that there are more positive ways to achieve respect and to get their voices heard.

Section Four contains longer activities, providing learning capsules to look in more depth at significant topics, including child sexual and criminal exploitation, knife crime and guns.

Throughout, step-by-step instructions are provided for each activity, which can be amended to meet different learning needs or to address local issues and concerns. Similarly, activities are flexible so they can be made longer or shorter than the times given as a guide, and there are signposts to additional information and support, which could be set as homework or extend learning outside of the group.

---

1   Children Act 1989, Section 105; Children Act 2004, Section 65.

Talking about emotive topics

Gangs and gang culture can be an emotive topic to discuss, for example people may have strong views on the right to carry a weapon for protection, 'stop and search' and the arguments for and against joint enterprise law. Make it clear that whilst expressing differences of opinion is to be encouraged, any actions that harass, scare or harm others are unacceptable and will not be tolerated.

Be sensitive to the life experiences that some young people may have. For some it will be the first time they have really considered gangs and gang culture whilst others may have first-hand experience of varying degrees. Many parents have strong views on gangs and may have been open in their condemnation, making it hard for young people to openly question some of the things they have seen and heard. This, along with the opinions of family, friends and community leaders, will have informed young people's understanding and shaped their views, both positively and negatively.

Agree the option to pass in discussions and not to participate in an activity if it becomes too much or is emotionally upsetting. Explain that young people will not be asked to share personal experiences and where appropriate signpost young people on to additional services for help and support. If a disclosure is made, follow safeguarding procedures and/or report to the police as appropriate.

Establishing a safe learning environment

Learning about gangs, gang-related behaviour and crime involves looking at a range of complex issues. Whilst the majority of young people will have no real life experience of gangs and gang-related crime, it is likely that they will have seen and heard things on social media, music videos, 'gangster' films, video games and traditional news sources, which may or may not be accurate.

Activities in this book deliberately use gender-neutral pronouns, apart from where specific case studies or examples are given. Similarly assumptions about ethnicity, class and ability are challenged to make the point that young people can be vulnerable to criminal and sexual exploitation for many reasons and from all backgrounds.

To ensure that everyone feels safe participating, take time to explain boundaries and limits to confidentiality, explaining when information would need to be passed on and what can 'stay in the room'. To help with this, ensure that there is a robust set of ground rules in place before starting, and refer back to them as work progresses. These may include:

- the right to feel safe

- freedom to express opinions and values

- the right to respectfully challenge

- the promotion of inclusion and diversity

- to listen without interrupting

- to ask questions to help learning

- to keep information confidential (within the boundaries discussed).

Supporting vulnerable young people

Whilst all young people are potentially at risk of being drawn into gangs, some are more vulnerable than others. Most research suggests that these more vulnerable young people include those:

- not involved in gangs, but living in an area where gangs are active

- not involved in gangs, but at risk of becoming victims of gangs

- not involved in gangs, but at risk of becoming drawn in by, for example siblings, partners or children of known gang members or

- gang-involved and at risk of harm through their gang-related activities (e.g. drug supply, weapon use, child sexual exploitation (CSE), trafficking and risk of attack from own or rival gang members).

Similarly Adverse Childhood Experiences (ACEs[2]), including a lack of positive adult role models, witnessing domestic abuse, health inequalities, emotional, physical and sexual abuse and neglect, all contribute to making some children and young people more 'at risk' than others.[3]

Inclusive learning

Young people with disabilities can have additional vulnerabilities that make it important to safeguard them from the influence and impact of gangs.

The word 'disability' is a collective term for such a huge range of physical, sensory and mental disabilities, including 'invisible' disabilities such as diabetes and deafness, that it is impossible to prescribe for all. Along this continuum pupils will have different learning needs and abilities, as well as differing levels of experience and understanding of gangs and gang-related crime.

This resource is not specifically aimed at students with Special Educational Needs (SEN) but many of the ideas can be easily adapted, for example by swapping words for pictures, using a larger type font or inviting students to draw, not write, their discussions. In some of the activities specific additional suggestions have been included, whilst others will need individual adaptation.[4]

The law

Knives and the law

- It is illegal for a shop to sell any kind of knife to someone under the age of 18. This includes kitchen knives and even cutlery. Some knives, such as flick knives, are illegal for even adults to buy.

---

2   The term was originally developed in the US for the Adverse Childhood Experiences survey, which found that as the number of ACEs increased in the population studied, so did the risk of experiencing a range of health conditions in adulthood. There have been numerous other studies that have found similar findings, including in Wales and England.

3   To find out more about ACEs, go to www.healthscotland.scot/population-groups/children/adverse-childhood-experiences-aces/overview-of-aces

4   For more information, go to https://assets.publishing.service.gov.uk/government/uploads/system/uploads/attachment_data/file/189392/DCSF-00064-2010.pdf.pdf

- It is illegal to carry a knife (regardless of whether a person says it is for their own protection or if they are carrying it for someone else).

- Possession of a knife can mean up to four years in prison, even if it is not used.

- Causing the death of someone with a knife can lead to a life sentence in prison.

Guns and the law

- It is illegal for a shop to sell guns (including imitation guns) to anyone under 18 years old, or to sell realistic imitation guns to anyone.

- It is illegal to carry a gun (regardless of whether a person says it is for their own protection or if they are carrying it for someone else).

- Possession of a gun can mean a minimum five-year sentence.

- Causing the death of someone with a gun can lead to a life sentence in prison.

Weapons and the law

- An offensive weapon is any object that has been made or adapted to cause injury or is carried with the intention of causing injury. This covers anything from purpose-built weapons such as guns and knives, to snooker cues, baseball bats and crutches.

Anti-social behaviour and the law

- Many things that constitute anti-social behaviour are also criminal offences, and people who commit them may be arrested. Committing anti-social behaviour may lead to receiving an acceptable behaviour contract, an Anti-Social Behaviour Order (ASBO), fines or a prison sentence.

- An ASBO sets out rules that a person must adhere to. It is not a criminal record, but if the terms of the ASBO are breeched, the law has been broken and further action will be taken. This is likely to mean being arrested and a possible prison sentence.[5]

Dogs and the law

- Some gang members use dogs to intimidate others and/or assist in things like drug deals and debt collection. These are sometimes referred to as 'weapon dogs'.

- This is illegal under the Dangerous Dogs Act 2014, which applies to all dogs regardless of breed or size.

- Under the Act, which strengthens previous acts, it's illegal for a dog to be 'dangerously out of control' or to bite or attack someone in a public place or within

---

5   See www.safe.met.police.uk

the home. The legislation also makes it an offence if a person is scared that a dog may bite them.

- It is also an offence for a dog to attack an assistance dog (Guide Dog, Hearing Dog, etc.). This may be considered a hate crime.

- Where a dog is used in the commission of any offence, it is subject to forfeiture by the courts under section 143 of the Powers of Criminal Courts (Sentencing) Act 2000. [6]

Reporting concerns

Parents, carers, family members and professionals in children's and young people's lives have an important role to play in helping protect them from gangs and keeping them away from violence. To ensure the safeguarding of children and young people and to develop effective multi-agency working, early intervention is key in identifying the most vulnerable and at risk.

Like other public bodies, schools and services for young people have a legal duty to prevent crime. If you have knowledge that a crime is about to be committed or believe a young person is at immediate risk of harm or poses an immediate risk to others, call 999.

If you consider that a young person is vulnerable or 'at risk' of gang-related activity, then assess any additional support needs and follow safeguarding protocols. Check with your line manager and record everything.

Report inappropriate content to social media providers and encourage young people to do the same (see 'Links to useful organizations and resources' below).

Linked books

Other books I have written that explore the gang-related topics of drugs, alcohol, pornography and relationships in more detail include:

- *Let's Talk Relationships: Activities for Exploring Love, Sex, Friendship and Family with Young People* (2010)

- *We Need to Talk about Pornography: A Resource to Educate Young People about the Potential Impact of Pornography and Sexualised Images on Relationships, Body Image and Self-Esteem* (2016)

- *A Little Book of Drugs: Activities to Explore Drug Issues with Young People* (2012)

- *A Little Book of Alcohol: Activities to Explore Alcohol Issues with Young People* (2012)

- *A Little Book of Tobacco: Activities to Explore Smoking Issues with Young People* (2012)

- *Working with Young Men: Activities for Exploring Personal, Social and Emotional Issues* (2006)

- *Working with Young Women: Activities for Exploring Personal, Social and Emotional Issues* (2010)

---

6   See https://www.cps.gov.uk/legal-guidance/dangerous-dog-offences https://www.rspca.org.uk/getinvolved/campaign/bsl/dda

- *101 Things to Do on the Street: Games and Resources for Detached, Outreach and Street-Based Youth Work* (2011)

Links to useful organizations and resources

Childline: www.childline.org.uk

Children and Young People Trafficked for the Purpose of Criminal Exploitation in Relation to County Lines: A Toolkit for Professionals, Joint report by the National Police Chief's Council, The Children's Society and Victim Support: www.csepoliceandprevention.org. uk/sites/default/files/Exploitation%20Toolkit.pdf

Gangsline: www.gangsline.com

Growing Against Violence (GAV): http://growingagainstviolence.org.uk

Home Office (2018) *Criminal Exploitation of Children and Vulnerable Adults: County Lines*, July: www.gov.uk/government/publications/criminal-exploitation-of-children-and-vulnerable-adults-county-lines

Metropolitan Police: www.met.police.uk

National Crime Agency (2017) *County Lines Violence, Exploitation and Drug Supply*, National Briefing Report, November: www.nationalcrimeagency.gov.uk/who-we-are/publications/234-county-lines-violen-ce-exploitation-drug-supply-2017/file

Redthread: www.redthread.org.uk

Runaway Helpline: www.runawayhelpline.org.uk

Stand Against Violence: http://standagainstviolence.co.uk

Key vocabulary

Below is a table listing common terms, acronyms and words used throughout this book. It may be helpful for teachers and youth workers to read to become familiar with any unknown vocabulary. It can also be shared with young people, where appropriate, who may want to offer suggestions for local meaning or even add new terms/words.

Vocabulary	Meaning
ACEs	Adverse Childhood Experiences are stressful events that occur in childhood
ASBO	Anti-Social Behaviour Order
CAMHS	Child and Adolescent Mental Health Services
CCE	Child criminal exploitation
CJS	Criminal justice system
CLA	Children looked after
County lines	Where children or young people are groomed and then internally trafficked for the purpose of criminal exploitation, which is a form of abuse
CSE	Child sexual exploitation

DfE	Department for Education
DH	Department of Health
Gay	A man who is sexually, physically and romantically attracted to the same gender; often also used to describe women attracted to women
Gender identity	The internal perception someone has of their gender and how they label themselves
Indecent image	As defined by legislation for England and Wales that deals directly with offences concerning indecent images of children: The Protection of Children Act 1978, Section 1 The Criminal Justice Act 1988, Section 160
LGBTQ+	This acronym is used as an inclusive term for those identifying as lesbian, gay, bisexual, transgender or questioning PLUS any other non-heterosexuals
Media	Online and traditional sources of news and information
NHS	National Health Service
Naked selfie	Sometimes called 'nudes' or 'glampics', this refers to intimate and/or erotic selfies usually taken for the purpose of sexual arousal. They are often sent via text or instant messaging, but can be kept by the owner. It is illegal to take, possess and share them if the person is under 18
Partner	Relationship partner of any gender
PCT	Primary Care Trust, responsible for commissioning health services
Pornography	Sexually explicit material for the primary purpose of sexual arousal; porn is the abbreviation
PSHE	Personal, Social and Health Education
Revenge porn	The distribution of a private sexual image of someone without their consent and with the intention of causing them distress
Selfie	A self-portrait taken with a mobile phone, usually to send to someone else or post on social media; these can be taken alone or with others
SEN	Special Educational Need
Sexting	Sending messages, usually by text, of a sexual nature
Sexual consent	Currently, the legal definition is that the individual must be over the age of 16 and able to understand the nature of the sex act and its consequences, there must be no pressure used, and they must be able to communicate their decision to have sex
Sexual orientation	The type of sexual, romantic and physical attraction someone feels for another person, usually based on gender
Social media	Websites and applications that enable users to create and share content or to participate in social networking; this includes Facebook, Instagram and Twitter
STI	Sexually transmitted infection (now used in preference to STD, sexually transmitted disease)
Stereotype	A stereotype is a commonly held belief about a person or group of people based on an assumption or incomplete knowledge, and then widely applied – for example, all women are bad drivers, all men like football. This can lead to prejudice and discrimination

Trans	An umbrella term to describe people whose gender is not the same as, or does not sit comfortably with, the sex they were assigned at birth. Trans people may describe themselves using one or more of a wide variety of terms, including (but not limited to) transgender, transsexual, gender-queer (GQ), gender-fluid, non-binary, gender-variant, crossdresser, genderless, agender, nongender, third gender, bi-gender, trans man, trans woman, trans masculine, trans feminine and neutrois[7]
YOT	Youth Offending Team

---

7   www.stonewall.org.uk/help-advice/faqs-and-glossary/glossary-terms#t

Section One

DEFINING GANGS

ACTIVITY 1: WHAT IS A GANG?

Aim

- To explore young people's existing knowledge of gangs and provide a starting point for understanding the term 'gang'.

Time: 30 minutes

Key vocabulary

- Gang
- Media
- Crime

You will need

- Flipchart paper and marker pens
- A4 paper and pens

How to do it

1. Divide the young people into groups and give each group some flipchart paper and enough marker pens for each group member to have one each. Ask a volunteer from each group to write the word 'Gang' in large letters in the middle of the paper.

2. Set a 2-minute task of each person writing as many related words, descriptions or messages to explain the word. This should create a 'wordstorm' of thoughts and ideas.

3. Call time and set another 2-minute challenge. Ask each group to come up with a short definition to explain what a 'gang' is, based on the wordstorm they made.

4. Announce time is up and in turn invite each group to stand up and present their 'gang' definition.

   Then share the following definitions:

   > The definition of a gang is a group of people with a shared interest, or who share a common identity.[1]

   > A gang is usually considered to be a group of people who spend time in public places that see themselves (and are seen by others) as a noticeable group, and engage in a range of criminal activity and violence.[2]

   Compare and contrast these definitions with the suggestions made by the young people, making the point that the word 'gang' can mean different things to different people. For example:

   - a 'crew' that breaks the law

   - a criminal organization in which the law is broken regularly

   - a group of friends hanging around in the street, parks or shopping centres.

   In particular highlight how the term 'gang' has come to have criminal connotations, particularly when used in the media.

---

1   PSHE & Citizenship, BBC Three – My Murder, 'Gang culture – the facts.' Available at www.bbc.co.uk/schools/pshe_and_citizenship/pdf/mymurder_resources/handout4.pdf

2   Bedfordshire Police, 'What is a gang?' Available at www.bedfordshire.police.uk/information-and-services/Advice/Gangs/What-is-a-gang

Ask: How might you know that someone is a member of a gang? Encourage discussions about how someone might be identified as belonging to one gang as opposed to another as well as any distinguishing behaviour and/or attitudes. This could include:

- using the gang name as part of their identity
- graffiti tags that members use to show their territory
- wearing 'colours', that is, clothes that symbolize membership
- a gang design tattoo
- initiation ceremonies
- promotion of shared beliefs (e.g. on social media, YouTube videos)
- music
- language
- codes.

Point out that it isn't just young people who join gangs; some adults join gangs too. Membership can be generational, with older family members having gang involvement or loyalties to gang members from previous associations.

ACTIVITY 2: GANGS, BUSTING THE MYTHS

Aim

- To challenge common gang myths, particularly those perpetuated in popular culture, and encourage wider discussion.

Time: 30 minutes

Key vocabulary

- Gangs
- Crime
- Violence
- Child criminal exploitation (CCE)
- Child sexual exploitation (CSE)

You will need

- A copy of the Myth or Fact Quiz
- A4 paper and pens
- Internet access

How to do it

1. Use the Myth or Fact Quiz to facilitate a prompt discussion to check out the information that young people have heard about gangs and gang culture. Give the quiz and a pen to each young person and ask them to complete it without conferring.

2. Go through the answers to the quiz, encouraging discussion as you go along. Use a distancing technique to further explore notions of protection and loyalty offered by gang membership, for example, 'If a young person is...' or 'How might a young person feel if...?' Suggest that many notions of gang life are informed by films, music and/or the media, and are not reality.

   Make the following points:

   - Most young people do not belong to a gang and never will do.

   - Being in a gang does not automatically protect you from harm. In fact, there is research that shows it makes you more likely to become a victim or target for crime.

   - Some researchers think that there are specific risks and vulnerabilities that make a young person more susceptible to gangs than their peers. However, just because you are at risk doesn't mean you will definitely join a gang.

3. Finally, invite the young people to go online to see the work that ex-gang members are doing to promote positive choices about gangs and violent crime. These organizations provide a starting point:

   - BoxUpCrime: http://boxupcrime.org/services/boxup-mentors

   - Gangsline: www.gangsline.com

   - Unity in the Community: www.unityinthecommunity.org.uk

MYTH OR FACT QUIZ

Have a look at the following statements and decide if you think it is a 'Myth' (M) or 'Fact' (F):

		M	F
1	Gangs are a recent phenomenon		
2	Belonging to a gang is against the law		
3	Only young people join gangs		
4	Joining a gang puts you more at risk of being involved in criminal activity		
5	Hooks like cash, clothes and mobiles are always used to tempt young people into gang life		
6	Gang membership offers access to a luxury lifestyle		
7	If you are arrested and convicted, the police and courts can seize any proceeds of crime, for example, cars, property and money		
8	Being in a gang offers you and your family protection		
9	Girls don't join gangs		
10	Only girls and young women are sexually exploited by gangs		
11	If you get arrested the gang will protect you as long as you keep your mouth shut		
12	Once you've joined a gang there is no way out		

Myth or Fact answers

1. Gangs are a recent phenomenon. **Myth:** Gangs are nothing new; they have been part of history for over 2000 years. From street gangs in Roman times to the 'Peaky Blinders' of the 20th century and the notorious Kray gang in 1960s London to those of today, the UK has a long history of criminal gang activity.

2. Belonging to a gang is against the law. **Myth:** Being in a gang is not a crime in itself. The term 'gang' can also be used to describe a group of friends, but criminal gangs tend to be more widely reported in the media.

3. Only young people join gangs. **Myth:** It's not just young people who join gangs; some adults do too. Membership can be generational, with older family members having gang involvement or old loyalties to gang members from previous associations.

4. Joining a gang puts you more at risk of being involved in criminal activity. **Fact:** According to research.[3]

5. Hooks like cash, clothes and mobiles are always used to tempt young people into gang life. **Myth:** Whilst incentives can be used, it's not that simple. Young people choose to join gangs for lots of different reasons, not just because they are given things. Some become involved via a relationship with a gang member, romantic or otherwise; others join because it's expected where they live; and others still are attracted to what they believe a criminal lifestyle offers. Enticing children and young people into a criminal gang is a form of child criminal exploitation (CCE).

6. Gang membership offers access to a luxury lifestyle. **Myth:** Whilst those at the top of a criminal network might get rich on the proceeds of crime, those at the bottom of the chain are unlikely to. Gang leaders and 'elders' will get the biggest cut at a local level with younger members often

---

3 Medina, J., Cebulla, A., Ross, A., Shute, J. and Aldridge, J. (2013) *Children and Young People in Gangs: A Longitudinal Analysis.* London: Nuffield Foundation. Available at www.nuffieldfoundation.org/sites/default/files/files/Children_young_people_gangs.pdf

relying on them for what they can get. Whilst any money may look initially tempting, it's worth remembering that whatever promises are made, there is no way of enforcing them if the money is not legally earned.

7. If you are arrested and convicted, the police and courts can seize any proceeds of crime, for example, cars, property and money. **Fact:** Whilst in gangster films criminals get around this by putting their assets in the name of their partners or a company, in the UK, the Proceeds of Crime Act 2002[4] closed this loophole and provides for the confiscation or civil recovery of any proceeds of crime. This means you could do a long prison sentence and come out with nothing, no matter how much you had.

8. Being in a gang offers you and your family protection. **Myth:** Gang membership has been linked to a rise in violent crime amongst young people, particularly gun and knife crime. It could make you a target for rival gangs and lead to losing existing friendships outside of the gang if friends choose not to get involved. It can also have negative effects on families, from reports of family members being targeted to younger siblings being singled out for recruitment.

9. Girls don't join gangs. **Myth:** Although their role within a gang can be different to those of young men, for example, some girls enter gang life through a romantic relationship with a gang member, others are used as lookouts, to entrap rival gang members or to carry drugs or cash in the belief that they are less likely to be stopped by the police. This is a form of sexual exploitation.

10. Only girls and young women are sexually exploited by gangs. **Myth:** Both young men and young women are at risk of sexual exploitation within gangs, for example, in exchange for protection or status, trafficking to pay off debts or to initiate new members into the gang. Sexual assault can also be used as a weapon to intimidate, blackmail or bully. It is a form child sexual abuse and can be used to control and coerce young people.

11. If you get arrested the gang will protect you as long as you keep your mouth shut. **Myth:** Whilst it might work this way in the films, there is no evidence to suggest that gang loyalty is automatically given. If you get a custodial sentence, gang membership might make you a target for violence, bullying or sexual abuse by rival gangs, and there is no guarantee that the gang will be waiting for you when you get out. Think hard before deciding to cover for someone else; be loyal to yourself and true to your values, and make the decision that is best for you.

12. Once you've joined a gang there is no way out. **Myth:** Whilst it might not be as easy as simply walking away, people can and do leave gangs to make different life choices. Some ex-gang members are now successfully acting as positive role models and mentors to help young people escape and live healthy, happy, gang-free lives.

---

4   www.legislation.gov.uk/ukpga/2002/29/contents

ACTIVITY 3: EXPLORING GANG STEREOTYPES

Aims

- To identify and describe examples of stereotypes related to gangs and crime.
- To understand the negative impact these stereotypes can have on society and individuals.
- To consider ways to effectively challenge stereotypes.

Time: 45 minutes

Key vocabulary

- Gang member
- Crime
- Stereotype
- Prejudice
- Discrimination

You will need

- Large sheets of paper and marker pens
- Copies of the Guess Who worksheet
- Glue sticks
- A copy of the poem 'How Does It Feel to Be Misperceived?' by George The Poet[5]

How to do it

1. Divide the young people into small groups and give each group a Guess Who worksheet, a large sheet of paper and a selection of marker pens.

2. Explain that amongst the silhouettes on the worksheet is a member of a renowned criminal gang. Tell them that this person has a police record for dealing drugs and common assault during a fight with a rival gang. The task for each group is to identify the person from their silhouette and then devise a profile for them to include their name, age and other personal details.

3. Once this is done, give out glue sticks and instruct a volunteer from each group to stick the completed profile in the middle of the large sheet of paper. They now have 10 minutes to create a web diagram around it using as many adjectives or short phrases as they can think of to describe what they think the gangster does and what gang life is like.

4. Invite feedback, comparing and contrasting different suggestions as you go along.

   Ask: What did you base your picture on? In particular, consider the gender, ethnicity and age of those identified as a ' gangster'; ask where these assumptions came from and whether it was a trusted source.

5. Ask the young people to reflect on a first impression that later turned out to be wrong and a time where they felt misjudged. Encourage discussion (avoiding anything that is painful or still unresolved) to consider how it feels to make a wrong judgement about somebody and the emotions when the same is done to them. Examples could include:

   - hurt

---

5   See https://genius.com/George-the-poet-how-does-it-feel-to-be-misperceived-annotated

 - frustrated

 - angry

 - misunderstood

 - resentful.

Ask: If these stereotypes are further reinforced in the media, how might it affect societal attitudes and behaviour? *For example, if you fit the stereotype you must be a gangster etc.*

6. Return to the Guess Who worksheet. Explain that the gang member is a young man called Billy and read out this scenario:

I got so sick of people assuming I must be a gang member just because of where I live and how I look. It made me angry. It wasn't just adults in the community; I got stopped by the police regularly even though I hadn't done anything. After what felt like the hundredth time, I gave in. If everyone thinks you are a gangster you may as well get the benefits of being one, right?

Facilitate a short discussion about Billy's decision to join a gang, even though he had been resisting it. Ask: What benefits might he perceive in joining the gang? *For example, acceptance, a sense of belonging, respect etc.*

Explain that there is research to suggest that labelling people and perpetuating stereotypes can lead to people accepting those labels and owning them. In Billy's case he became so angry and frustrated at being misrepresented that he sought acceptance and validation from his local gang.

7. Back in small groups, give out copies of the poem 'How Does It Feel to Be Misperceived?' to read and discuss. The poem is by George Mpanga, better known by his stage name George The Poet, a London-born spoken word performer of Ugandan heritage, known for his work with Wretch 32, Naughty Boy, Krept & Konan and Mikill Pane, amongst others.

Ask: What is the poem about? *For example, inequality, injustice, assumptions made based on stereotypes etc.* What do you think he means by 'Just consider this/My life could have been your life with a twist'?

According to annotation by George The Poet he's pointing out that basically we are all the same, we all want the same good things in life and to achieve, but for some there is less of an opportunity.

8. Conclude by stressing the importance of not making assumptions based on stereotypes about gangs. Just because a young person lives in a certain area, dresses a certain way or likes a certain type of music this doesn't mean that they are in a gang or will commit gang-related crime. Artists like George The Poet challenge these stereotypes through their work and encourage others to have their say to raise the profile of their community and gain respect in positive ways.

GUESS WHO

ACTIVITY 4: MEDIA WATCH

Aims

- To demonstrate that concerns about young people and gangs is not a new phenomenon.

- To explore the language used in news stories featuring young people, gangs and crime.

- To consider the impact this might have on societal assumptions made about all young people.

Time: 60 minutes

Key vocabulary

- Media stereotypes

- Gangs

- Young people

You will need

- Sticky notes, flipchart paper and pens

- A set of Media Headlines

- A selection of current news articles about youth gangs and/or gang-related crime (taken from a reputable news source)

How to do it

1. Give each young person a sticky note and a pen. Ask them to write one word on it (or a couple of words) to describe how gangs are represented in the media today. Instruct them to fold the note up without showing anyone, until you ask them to later.

2. Take the set of Media Headlines. These are a selection of headlines from different newspapers printed over the last 50 years. Explain that there is no date on any of the headlines as the group task is to try to put them in the correct chronological order (on the floor or wall).

   Allow 10 minutes for this, encouraging volunteers to place the headlines in date order, with an explanation as to why they think this is correct.

   Correct slide order:

   - Headline 1 = 2019[6]

   - Headline 3 = 2018[7]

   - Headline 5 = 2014[8]

   - Headline 7 = 2009[9]

---

6   Newman, J. (2019) '"Despicable" teenage yobs are slammed for punching and kicking an ambulance as paramedics on a 999 call tried to treat patient inside.' *Daily Mail*, 27 April. Available at www.dailymail.co.uk/news/article-6966509/Teenage-yobs-punch-kick-ambulance-paramedics-treat-patient-inside.html

7   Gillespie, T. (2018) '"Kids walking around with knives" Feral youths holding TERRIFIED town to ransom.' *Express*, 29 January. Available at www.express.co.uk/news/uk/911383/Hyde-Tameside-Greater-Manchester-kids-knives

8   Peacock, L. (2014) 'The dark side of female empowerment: The rise of Britain's "gangster girls" running gangs.' *The Telegraph*, 28 May. Available at www.telegraph.co.uk/women/womens-life/10857716/Britains-gangster-girls-The-dark-side-of-female-empowerment-The-rise-of-women-and-females-running-gangs.html

9   Chapman, J. (2009) 'A nation of bad parents: Britain's youngsters are among the worst for drinking, smoking and teenage pregnancy, warns the OECD.' *Daily Mail*, 2 September. Available at www.dailymail.co.uk/news/article-1210438/UK-teenage-girls-worst-drunks-world-despite-billions-spent-welfare.html

- Headline 8 = 1999[10]
- Headline 4 = 1981[11]
- Headline 2 = 1974[12]
- Headline 6 = 1958[13]

3. Once the young people believe they have the correct order, go through the headlines, inviting discussion and moving any that are incorrect to the right place. Inform the young people of the dates these events happened, demonstrating the time span of the news reports, reminding them that concern about gangs and gang-related crime is not new.

4. Divide the main group into four smaller groups, giving each group flipchart paper, pens and copies of the news articles you selected. Their new task is to read an article and then discuss it using the prompt questions below, noting key points to be raised back in the main group.

   - Who do you think the story is aimed at?

   - What words are used to describe the young people?

   - What are the key 'take home' messages?

   Allow up to 15 minutes and then bring everyone together. Each group can now feedback their findings. Encourage the young people to identify the type of language used in the articles, the style of stories and the messages given about the worth and value of young people.

   Ask: Do you think that reporting styles have changed much over the years?

   Consider the use of aggressive headlines – negative or subjective words could give rise to unhelpful stereotypes about all young people, and not just those who have been convicted of a crime. Have the words changed over the years? Has the meaning? Examples such as 'feral youth', 'drug-taking', 'youth violence', 'yob' or 'hoodie' would arguably suggest that young people are presented as a 'problem' for society rather than as equal members.

5. Now, ask each participant to unfold their sticky note and read out the word they wrote. How do these compare to the words used in the newspapers and online news sources?

6. Compare and contrast the words with the news headlines and those written up on flipchart paper capturing previous findings. If there are lots of similarities, facilitate discussion about how this makes them feel. Suggest that hearing negative things all the time can make some people feel the need to prove them wrong and others to feel that as they already have the 'name', they might as well live up to it.

7. Conclude by explaining that it has been argued that the media demonizes young people by only reporting the negative events or things they do rather than balancing bad press with the positive contributions they make, for example, volunteering, raising money, achieving goals etc. This can impact negatively on their position in society and fuel divisions, creating a 'blame' culture, giving people who don't have much contact with teenagers a negative impression, leading to fear and even anger.

10 Hickley, M. (1999) 'One in four adolescents is a criminal.' *Daily Mail*, September. Available at www.dailymail.co.uk/news/article-34916/One-adolescents-criminal.html

11 Williams, R. (1981) 'LOOTING BLITZ IN MOSS SIDE: "I saw 20 youths on the rampage."' *Manchester Evening News*, 8 July. Taken from '1981 Moss Side riots: Pictures, headline and background that tell the story of some of Manchester's most violent days.' Available at www.manchestereveningnews.co.uk/news/greater-manchester-news/moss-side-riots-anniversary-manchester-9588570

12 'School-leaving age blamed for rising teenage crime.' *Daily Mirror*, 25 March 1974. Available at www.british newspaperarchive.co.uk/search/results/1974-01-01/1974-12-31?basicsearch=teenage%20crime&exactsearch=false&retrievecountrycounts=false&newspapertitle=daily%2bmirror

13 *Sunday Dispatch* (June 1958) 'Teddy boys terrified trippers.' Taken from Staveley-Wadham, R. (2020) 'Hooligans and gangsters? A look at the Teddy Boys of the 1950s.' The British Newspaper Archive, 7 April. Available at https://blog.britishnewspaperarchive.co.uk/2020/04/07/a-look-at-the-teddy-boys-of-the-1950s

MEDIA HEADLINES

Headline 1: '"Despicable" teenage yobs are slammed for punching and kicking an ambulance as paramedics on a 999 call tried to treat patient inside'

Headline 2: 'School-leaving age blamed for rising teenage crime: Raising of the school leaving age was blamed by a police chief'

Headline 3: '"Kids walking around with knives!" Feral youths holding TERRIFIED town to ransom'

Headline 4: 'LOOTING BLITZ IN MOSS SIDE: "I saw 20 youths on the rampage"'

Headline 5: 'The dark side of female empowerment: The rise of Britain's "gangster girls" running gangs'

Headline 6: 'Teddy boys terrified trippers'

Headline 7: 'A nation of bad parents: Britain's youngsters amongst world's worst for drinking, smoking and teenage pregnancy'

Headline 8: 'One in four adolescents is a criminal'

ACTIVITY 5: TESTING THE VALIDITY

Aims

- To test the validity of news reporting on gangs and young people.
- To consider the impact 'fake news' can have on perceptions of gang activity.

Time: 45 minutes

Key vocabulary

- Media stereotypes
- Validity
- 'Fake news'
- Gangs
- Young people

You will need

- Copies of this article from *The Independent* newspaper (or similar): 'Forty years ago pictures of Mods and Rockers shocked polite society. But were they staged by the press?'[14]
- YouTube clip from the riot scene in the film *Quadrophenia*[15]
- Flipchart paper and pens

How to do it

1. Explain that having identified some of the negativity expressed in the media towards young people, you are now going to test the validity of a historical news report about young people and gangs.

   Show the clip from the 1979 film *Quadrophenia*, which features a re-enactment of the real-life 'Battle of Brighton Beach' between Mods and Rockers on a May Bank Holiday weekend back in 1964.

2. Give out copies of *The Independent* article (or enable young people to view it online). Divide the young people into groups to discuss the following (write the questions on flipchart paper):

   - Why do you think reporters/journalists/photographers at the time may have exaggerated the events? *For example, to increase readership of their newspaper, to make the story more shocking, to make themselves look good for staying in such a dangerous environment, to fit the existing narrative about teenagers and their behaviour etc.*

   - Do you think this type of 'fake news' could happen now? Ask them for examples and discuss why they think it is or isn't less likely to happen today. Prompt consideration of different types of media, including online media like Twitter and Instagram and more traditional forms like the print version of newspapers or TV news.

   - How do you think stories like this impact on how adults/communities view young people? Does it represent them in a good light, worthy of respect? Are they presented as valued

---

14 Stummer, R. (2004) 'Forty years ago pictures of Mods and Rockers shocked polite society. But were they staged by the press?' *The Independent*, 4 April. Available at www.independent.co.uk/news/media/forty-years-ago-pictures-of-mods-and-rockers-shocked-polite-society-but-were-they-staged-by-the-5354522.html
15 See www.youtube.com/watch?v=MrDlXGD6I1s

citizens or a 'drain' on society? Consider if some of the language used would be acceptable if applied to other groups in society, for example, the elderly or middle-aged.

3. It has been argued that the media demonizes young people by only reporting the negative events or things they do rather than balancing bad press with the positive contributions they make, for example, volunteering, raising money, achieving goals etc. This can impact negatively on their position in society and fuel divisions, creating a 'blame' culture, giving people who don't have much contact with teenagers a negative impression, leading to fear and even anger. Ask for any experiences participants may have had of being misjudged due to others' pre-conceptions and how this felt.

    Summarize that stereotypes perpetuated by the media can distort views of young people negatively, for example, that all young people are in gangs, commit crime and carry weapons. These untruths can lead to discrimination, in the workplace, access to health and other services etc.

4. Divide the young people into pairs and ask each pair to come up with an example of how stereotypes of young people, gangs and crime can impact negatively in other areas of life that affect all young people. These can be written down in the same style as the examples below:

    –   Stereotype example A: *All young people are lazy and want something for nothing*. Negative thinking that could lead to discrimination: young people think the world owes them a living. Potential discrimination: I wouldn't employ a young person because they will be unreliable and won't turn up.

    –   Stereotype example B: *Young women only get pregnant so they can get a flat*. Negative thinking that could lead to discrimination: a young woman living in social housing? I bet she only got that because she's a single parent. Potential discrimination: I'm not going to be friendly to my new neighbour. Other people deserve that flat more than her.

    –   Stereotype example C: *All young people take drugs*. Negative thinking that could lead to discrimination: that young person is acting strangely and stumbling about, I bet they're on drugs. Potential discrimination: I won't call for medical help; if they choose to take drugs it's their own fault if they pass out.

5. Facilitate a circle time that invites each pair to share their example. Conclude that online and offline media only tends to report on a small minority of young people, but that this influences how parents and other adults in the community view the majority. It can also impact on younger children who think that behaving in some of the extreme ways reported is normal, and potentially influences their thoughts and behaviour. Invite suggestions about ways that these can be challenged so that everyone gets the message that not all young people commit crime or join gangs.

ACTIVITY 6: GANGS, LEGAL OR ILLEGAL?

Aim

- To identify legal or illegal gang activity.

Time: 20 minutes

Key vocabulary

- Gang
- Legal
- Illegal

You will need

- Copies of the Legal or Illegal Quiz and pens

How to do it

1. This quiz can be completed in pairs or individually. Give out copies of the quiz and pens, and allow up to 10 minutes for the young people to complete it.

2. Call time and go through the quiz and answers, awarding a point for every correct answer. At the end ask the young people to check their score to see who has the most points.

3. Congratulate the winner and facilitate a discussion that considers the differences between a group of young people that regularly meet in a public space to hang out and have fun, and a gang. This should cover:

   - purpose of meeting up
   - activities
   - intent
   - perception of others.

LEGAL OR ILLEGAL QUIZ

Have a look at the gang-related activities below and decide if you think they are L = legal, P = potentially illegal or I = illegal.

	Activity	L	P	I
1	Smoking cannabis in a public place			
2	Keeping acid in a bottle to use as a weapon			
3	Training a dog			
4	Using social media to challenge a rival gang to a fight			
5	Using offensive language in a public place			
6	Meeting regularly in one postcode			
7	Liking grime artists			
8	Posting drill rap to trade insults with another gang on a music sharing platform			
9	Paying younger gang members to take drugs to different locations to deal (also known as 'county lines')			
10	Insulting a gang member's girlfriend on social media			
11	Threatening someone with a replica gun			
12	Looking after drugs money for a gang			
13	Having a relationship with a gang member			
14	Spraying graffiti tags on public buildings			
15	Making a noise in a public space			

Quiz answers

1	**Smoking cannabis in a public place**	Illegal
	Cannabis is a Class B drug. For possession you could receive up to five years in prison, an unlimited fine or both. For supply and production this rises to 14 years. You can be charged with possessing an illegal substance, even if it's not yours. If you are under 18 the police can tell your parent or the adult responsible for you.	
2	**Squirting acid from a bottle at someone**	Illegal
	After a rise in acid attacks many UK retailers have banned the sale of acid to under-18s. Under Section 18 of the Offences Against the Person Act 1861, acid attackers who intentionally carry and throw a corrosive substance at another person can face life imprisonment.	
3	**Training a dog**	Not illegal
	All responsible dog owners should train their dogs. However, gang members often breed dangerous dogs to facilitate drug deals and debt collection, as well as to enhance the gang's image. Allowing a dog to be 'dangerously out of control' is against the law on private property as well as in public.	
4	**Using social media to challenge a rival gang to a fight**	Not illegal
	Lots of groups use social media to arrange meet-ups and events, which is not illegal. However, the reason for the meet-up or what happens when the meeting takes place could be illegal.	

5	**Using offensive language in a public place** Someone (of any age) could be arrested for swearing in the street. There are several offences that could be committed involving abusive words or threatening behaviour. To decide if an offence has been committed things like the intention of the person swearing, if this is an ongoing disturbance, previous history etc. would all be considered. Someone is more likely to be arrested if the incident takes places in the presence of a police officer or police community support officer (PCSO).	Potentially illegal
6	**Meeting regularly in one postcode** It's not illegal to regularly meet anywhere unless to do so breaks a dispersal order or bylaw or is trespassing.	Not illegal
7	**Liking grime artists** But see below, number 8.	Not illegal
8	**Posting drill rap to trade insults with another gang on a music sharing platform** This is potentially illegal depending on the content and any threats to harm or kill contained in the lyrics. A gang was given a Criminal Behaviour Order (CBO) at Kingston Crown Court[16] forbidding them from referring to their own gang or rivals in their music. It also required them to allow the police to attend any of their performances.	Potentially illegal
9	**Paying younger gang members to take drugs to different locations to deal (also known as 'county lines')** Drug dealing is illegal and the penalties depend on the drugs sold. The term 'county lines' is used to describe gangs from large urban areas that travel to locations in county or coastal towns to sell class 'A' drugs. Gangs typically recruit and exploit children and vulnerable young people to courier drugs and cash as they are less likely to be suspected of breaking the law, and the real criminals can remain anonymous.	Illegal
10	**Insulting a gang member's girlfriend on social media** Posts can be upsetting or insulting or express an unpopular view but they are not necessarily criminal. If they are grossly offensive, inappropriate or malicious they could meet the threshold for prosecution. If anyone is threatened, harassed or bullied online they should report it to the service provider and/or the police.	Potentially illegal
11	**Threatening someone with a replica gun** It is illegal to carry a knife or a gun, even an imitation one. Anyone caught in possession will be arrested and prosecuted.	Illegal
12	**Looking after drugs money for a gang** However, the Modern Slavery Act 2015 may provide opportunities to consider the circumstances of 'county line' offending, particularly where there has been deliberate targeting, recruitment and significant exploitation of young and vulnerable people.	Illegal
13	**Having a relationship with a gang member** Whilst it is not illegal, spending time with someone involved in criminal gang activity could increase the risk of law breaking or becoming a potential witness to illegal activity.	Not illegal
14	**Spraying graffiti tags on public buildings** Graffiti is an offence of criminal damage and, if prosecuted, the offender could face a fine or even imprisonment. Local authorities can issue fixed penalty notices for offences of graffiti. It is also an offence for under-16s to buy aerosol paint cans.	Illegal
15	**Making a noise in a public space** It's not illegal to have fun, play loud games or talk and joke in public. However, if this becomes too loud or impacts on other people's enjoyment of a public space, it may be considered anti-social behaviour and the police may be called.	Potentially illegal

---

16   Baynes, C. (2018) 'Drill rap gang banned from making music without police permission in legal first.' *The Independent*, 15 June. Available at www.independent.co.uk/news/uk/crime/drill-rap-gang-ban-music-videos-met-police-court-order-ladbroke-grove-a8400371.html

ACTIVITY 7: WHY DO PEOPLE JOIN GANGS?

Aims

- To better understand some of the reasons young people join a gang.
- To explore the expectations and realities of gang life.

Time: 20 minutes

Key vocabulary

- Gang
- Belonging
- Kudos
- Crime

You will need

- Sets of the Why Join a Gang? cards

How to do it

1. Divide the young people into small groups and give each group a set of Why Join a Gang? cards.

2. Explain that on each of the cards a young person gives a reason for joining a gang. The groups' task is to read the card, discuss what's on it and then agree whether they think this is the most likely reason or not. The cards should be ranked with the most likely at the top going down to the least.

3. Invite each group to share their findings, explaining why they have placed some reasons higher than others.

   Explain that whilst some may think that gang life will be exciting or rewarding, the reality can be very different. As well as the adrenaline highs of rule breaking, comradeship, the excitement of being part of something and any financial gain, research suggests that being part of a gang increases the risk of:

   - being asked to do things you don't want to do

   - committing crime

   - dealing, trafficking or taking drugs

   - a criminal record

   - violence or death.

WHY JOIN A GANG?

Power and status	To make money
Shared interests	Fear, intimidation or threats
To belong	Protection from rival gangs
Boredom	To be respected
To have a role	To fit in
To find role models	To break rules and take risks
Peer pressure	Because a friend, sibling or partner already belongs
Excitement	To have a purpose

ACTIVITY 8: GANG ASSUMPTIONS

Aims

- To explore assumptions made about belonging to a gang.
- To discuss positive ways of achieving a sense of identity and belonging.

Time: 30 minutes

Key vocabulary

- Gang
- Identity
- Confidence
- Pride

You will need

- A4 paper and pens
- Whiteboard or flipchart paper and marker pens

How to do it

1. Divide the young people into pairs, giving each a piece of paper and a pen. Read Jack's case study and then ask each couple to discuss the following and make notes:

   - What do you think Jack is talking about?
   - Who do you imagine he is describing? What do they look like?

Case study: Jack

I joined because where I live it's not safe to go out on your own at night. I got to hear about it through an older friend and although he didn't force me to join, what he was saying made it sound interesting and exciting.

   Now I have friends and people I can rely on. I'm loyal to them and wear their colours with pride. I'm not scared anymore because I know I can take care of myself.

   It's become such a big part of my life. I've proved myself and can't imagine giving it up now; it is part of my identity, who I am.

2. Stop and invite feedback, writing up suggestions as they are called out. At this stage accept all ideas and do not challenge or discuss.

3. Go on to ask the following:

   - Jack says it is now 'part of his identity'. What do you think he means?
   - Why might he feel 'pride' in belonging?

   Facilitate answers as a whole group discussion exploring notions of pride and how belonging has given Jack confidence.

   Reveal: Jack is describing joining a martial arts club, based at his local gym. Becoming fit, eating healthily and working towards different levels has given him a sense of purpose and increased his confidence. Having found something he is good at, Jack has competed at a local level and his goal is to represent his club at national events.

4. Return to the suggestions recorded from the first part of the exercise, and ask the young people to reflect on the assumptions they made and what informed them. These are likely to include:

    - media reports

    - personal beliefs

    - family values and attitudes

    - education

    - life experiences.

    Suggest that the benefits of gang life expressed by many also describe membership of more positive groups and clubs. Point out that there are legitimate ways to feel secure, confident and proud, and look at local opportunities that could provide these.

ACTIVITY 9: **SAME, BUT DIFFERENT**

Aims

- To introduce the concept of shared and individual identity.
- To explore how group thinking can influence behaviour, attitudes and values.

Time: 45 minutes

Key vocabulary

- Individual and group identity
- Group thinking and behaviour

You will need

- A lemon for each young person (or sweets, strawberries, nuts etc.)
- A basket to hold the lemons (or sweets, strawberries, nuts etc.)
- A4 paper and pens

How to do it

1. Ask each young person to choose a lemon (or alternative) from the basket. Tell them to look closely at the fruit, examine it for distinctive marks and feel the skin. Encourage them to personalize their lemon by naming it.

2. Next collect the lemons back into the basket and make a show of mixing the fruit up. Then spread all the lemons out on the floor and invite the young people in turn to come and collect the fruit they chose, the one that belongs to them. In the event there are any disputes over ownership, place the lemon to one side as 'unidentified'. These should be left over at the end for reuniting. Ask:

   - How sure are you that you claimed *your* lemon?
   - How can you tell?
   - What makes it different and unique?
   - Is there such a thing as a 'perfect' lemon?

3. Conclude that there is no such thing as perfect; just like the lemons we are all different and unique whilst also having the shared identity of being 'human'. Explain that we are now going to explore this further to better understand.

4. Give everyone a piece of A4 paper and a pen. Ask them to sign their name on it and write four things about themselves anywhere on the page. Encourage a move away from physical attributes to think about the inner things that make them unique, for example, likes/dislikes, beliefs and values, skills and qualities etc.

5. Call time and then instruct everyone to hold their paper up in front of them, and without speaking, to walk around the room to find others with similar things written down. Once they have found others with similar things, ask them to form groups of at least four and to sit down with their sheets of paper laid out together in front of them to discuss the things they have in common, selecting those they think are the most important, and adding additional things they have in common as their talk progresses.

6. Now they have found the things that unite them, set a new task to identify differences. Encourage them to share and celebrate these by explaining their importance. Suggest that these are the things that contribute to a person's 'individual identity', that is, what makes them unique.

7. Bring the group back together and invite each young person to introduce their group identity rather than the things that define them as individuals. Ask:

    –   What aspects of identity did you focus on to form your groups? *For example, shared values, a common goal, shared skills or interests.*

    –   Once formed, how easy was it to discover more things in common? *As groups form, individuals tend to look for similarities rather than differences, which strengthens the group identity and bonds members together.*

    –   What became more important, creating the group identity or maintaining your individual one? *Consider organizations that have a strong group or team identity, for example, the army, sports teams or uniformed organizations where the uniform signifies membership at a glance.*

    –   Why might group identity be important within a gang? *For example, creates a sense of belonging, pride, peer recognition, protection, security, safety etc.*

8. Conclude that all membership groups, formal or informal, are made up of individuals who come together for a common purpose. Discovering shared interests and beliefs brings people together and creates a sense of belonging and security, which, in turn, can raise self-esteem. As the group identity grows, showing outsiders who belongs to the group can become important, for example, wearing a uniform.

    Suggest that group thinking can influence the behaviour, attitudes and values of individuals in positive or negative ways, and invite examples.

ACTIVITY 10: IDENTITY AND BELONGING

Aim

- To explore identity and understand how the different groups we belong to inform our sense of self and shape our self-esteem.

Time: 30 minutes

Key vocabulary

- Individual, community and social identity
- Belonging and gang

You will need

- Flipchart paper and marker pens
- A4 paper
- Sticky notes

How to do it

1. Explain that this activity moves on from individual identity to look at how membership of a community influences behaviour and beliefs. This can be described as a 'community identity'. Ask the young people to call out things that they think bring people together to form a 'community identity'. This could include:

   - faith

   - culture

   - family

   - school/college/work

   - place you live

   - ethnicity

   - gender identity

   - sexual orientation

   - age.

   Ask: Can you assume these identities or do you have to be born into them?

2. On a large sheet of paper write up ideas under the two headings, 'Assume' and 'Born into'. Be aware that some may go across both columns, for example, you may be born into one faith but convert to another, but most will fit into one or the other.

3. After a short discussion, divide the young people into groups of four and give out flipchart paper and pens. This time ask them to think of groups that the young people belong to. These should be groups that contribute *positively* to someone's 'social identity', that is, that they feel affiliated to, that reflects their values, likes/dislikes etc. and contributes to how they want to be seen by others. These can be anything from a uniformed youth organization to a sports team to a group on social media.

   Ideas should be explored on flipchart paper under the following headings:

   - group (name of group or collective description, for example, Scouts)

- identification (things group members wear, say or do to demonstrate membership, for example, a Scouts uniform)

- what you gain from membership (what someone gets or can achieve from belonging, for example, friendship, shared interests, opportunities to learn new skills and work towards Scouts badges etc.)

- what you give in return (for example, commitment, time and loyalty to your Scout troop).

Allow up to 30 minutes for discussions and then invite the groups to present one idea at a time, encouraging questions and discussion as you go along.

4. Facilitate a whole group discussion that invites the young people to reflect on the different groups they belong to using the following prompt questions:

- What groups do you belong to?

- How do they influence who you are?

- Do you behave differently in different groups? If so, how?

5. Conclude that individuals can belong to one or more groups, reflecting the different interests they have. Within each group, their individual identity contributes to a group identity, which becomes a blend of all members and the things they have in common, for example, shared values, beliefs and aspirations. New members are likely to try to fit in with the culture of the group and adopt the things that identify them as part of it. In some cases this is formalized into a ceremony where members pledge to sign up to the shared vision and abide by the group rules, for example, joining the Air Cadets or Guides.

ACTIVITY 11: GROUP MEMBERSHIP VS. GANG MEMBERSHIP

Aims

- To consider similarities and differences between group and gang membership.
- To better understand why some young people join gangs.

Time: 20 minutes

Key vocabulary

- Membership
- Identity
- Belonging
- Difference

You will need

- Sticky notes and pens

How to do it

1. Ask: What's the difference between a member of a group and a member of a gang? Explain that this is what you are going to explore now.

2. In pairs, ask the young people to come up with 10 similarities and 10 differences and write them onto sticky notes. Give them up to 15 minutes to complete the task and stick their ideas on the wall in two separate areas. These could include:

Similarities	Differences
A sense of belonging	Not breaking any laws in a group
An identity	Gangs seen as outside society
Shared experiences	Unlikely to be harmed or harm others in a group
Security/safety	Gang rivalry
Friends	Can be hard to leave a gang
Something to do	Gang links to weapons
Loyalty	Negative media images of gangs
Respect	Perceptions by family/community
Has rules	Disrespect for non-gang members
Provides role models	Harder to say no in a gang

3. Once these have been stuck on the wall, begin to cluster similar ideas together. As a whole group review suggestions, looking at things like the concept of respect and what it means within both contexts.

Example: respect

Gang = 'respect' can mean 'feared' based on a reputation for aggressive behaviour or violence. Once gained, having the respect of gang members can provoke the need to preserve it, which can lead to more extreme behaviour. Being 'disrespected' is seen as a something worthy of punishment and revenge.

Group = 'respect' in this context is much more likely to mean respecting that people have differing points of view based on a range of things including faith, culture, gender and life experience and a right to be who they are without judgement. Showing respect would include listening, empathy and celebrating diversity.

4. Conclude that whilst there are similarities in what can be gained from both group membership and becoming part of a gang, there are some fundamental differences. These include the increased risk of being harmed or getting involved in criminal activity, which could lead to a criminal record and other consequences that negatively impact on the life choices someone can make.

Section Two

RISK TAKING

ACTIVITY 12: TAKING RISKS

Aim

- To explore the concept of risk and risk-taking behaviour.

Time: 30 minutes

Key vocabulary

- Risk
- Risk factors
- Long- and short-term risk

You will need

- A set of Risk cards
- 2 sheets of A4 paper, headed: 'Very risky' and 'Not very risky'

How to do it

1. Wordstorm with the young people what is meant by 'risk' and devise a group definition. *For example, a typical dictionary definition of risk is 'a situation involving exposure to danger'.*

2. Seat everyone in a circle and hand each person a Risk card. Place one of the A4 sheets on one side of the circle where everyone can see it and the other on the opposite side.

3. In turn invite the young people to read out what is on their card and then place it between the A4 sheets to show how risky or not they consider the activity. Encourage the young people to explain their decision, setting a rule that other group members cannot challenge the placing of cards until later.

4. Go around the circle until all the cards have been used, and then ask if anyone wants to move any of the cards. Explain that all risks are relative, for example, some are likely to cause damage to health, some may not pose a serious risk but some may be very dangerous. Some effects of risky behaviour are immediate, that is, short-term risk, but some may not become obvious for years, that is, longer-term risk. *For example, joining a gang may not be an immediate risk but membership could lead to participation in higher-risk activities, which increases risk to self and others later on.*

5. Facilitate a discussion that considers what factors might add to these risks. *For example, peer pressure, wanting to fit in, the promise of excitement or the lure of easy money, judgements influenced by alcohol or drugs.*

RISK

Joining a gang	Getting into a car you know is stolen
Making friends with older peers	Lying about your age
Watching pornography	Walking home alone at night
Lying to parents/carers about where you are	Getting drunk with friends in a park
Having unprotected sex	Playing violent online games
Starting a fight	Defending a friend in a street fight
Accepting gifts from unknown adults	Binge drinking alcohol
Disobeying curfews set by parents/carers	Regularly smoking cannabis
Running errands for cash	Lying to parents/carers about who you spend time with
Skipping lessons to stay home	Missing school to be with older friends
Travelling alone on public transport	Mixing prescription drugs with alcohol to get drunk quicker
Borrowing money you can't pay back	Hiding a weapon for someone else
Crossing the road without looking	Hanging out with friends who break the law
Carrying a knife for protection	

ACTIVITY 13: ATTITUDES TO RISK

Aims

- To explore attitudes to taking risks.
- To consider the likely consequences of choices made.

Time: 20 minutes

Key vocabulary

- Risks
- Attitudes
- Choices
- Consequences

You will need

- Sticky notes and pens
- Flipchart paper and marker pens

How to do it

1. Divide the young people into pairs and give each pair five sticky notes and a pen. Ask them to identify five risk-taking activities that are generally admired in the UK, for example, parachute jumping for charity, diving, mountain climbing, skiing, sailing around the world etc. One risk should be written on each sticky note.

2. When they have completed the task, invite one person from each pair to read it out in turn and then stick their suggestions onto a designated space on the wall. Ask the young people to identify and cluster duplicates together.

3. As a whole group start to move the activities into a continuum of the most to least risky activities, asking what makes something more or less dangerous as you go along. Now ask for ways to make the activities less risky, for example, learning how to parachute jump, doing a practice jump with a qualified instructor, wearing protective clothing, checking the weather before you do it, conducting last minute safety checks etc.

4. Now, draw a dividing line down a sheet of flipchart paper and ask the young people to call out suggestions for risk-taking activities not admired by society, for example, fighting, carrying a weapon, taking drugs etc. Write these up on the left-hand side of the paper as they are called out.

    Ask: What is the difference between these risky behaviours and those already considered? Write up ideas in the column on the right, for example, these risk-taking activities are usually unplanned, may cause harm to self or others, could result in a criminal record etc. Conclude that whilst there is danger in both types of risks, which could ultimately lead to an accident or even death, before doing an extreme sports activity a risk assessment is conducted so things can be put in place to reduce risk to an acceptable level. If health and safety standards are not met, the activity doesn't go ahead. In contrast, risky behaviour is often impulsive or fuelled by anger; it can be a result of peer pressure or misguided notions of loyalty, and can happen without considering the full consequences.

    Suggest that whilst a formal risk assessment may not always be possible, it is important to think through the possible consequences of any risk-taking activity before deciding whether to go ahead. Developing the skills to think ahead and teaching yourself to question if a potentially negative consequence is really worth it is likely to reduce the likelihood of putting yourself and/ or others in danger.

ACTIVITY 14: ATTITUDES TO CRIME

Aims

- To explore different attitudes to crime and criminal activity.
- To consider the potential consequences of engaging in criminal behaviour.

Time: 30 minutes

Key vocabulary

- Attitudes
- Values
- Crime
- Consequences

You will need

- Copies of the Attitudes to Crime worksheet
- Pens

How to do it

1. Start by explaining that this activity explores attitudes to criminal activity; it is not asking young people to inform on each other or to speculate on the behaviour of others.

2. Hand each young person a copy of the Attitudes to Crime worksheet and a pen, and ask them to quietly complete it on their own. When everyone has finished, go through the worksheet, inviting the young people to share their opinions. Suggest that whilst some statements definitely describe criminal behaviour, for example, making online threats (including those of a sexual nature), carrying a knife, buying a replica weapon, giving a false statement to the police and benefiting financially from the proceeds of crime, other activities are not in themselves a crime but could easily escalate into law breaking, for example, defending yourself, holding extreme views, associating with criminals. Make it clear that in the UK everyone has the democratic right to support a cause and to stand up for what they believe in, but not if this oppresses others and their rights to feel safe and to express their own views.

3. In pairs, ask the young people to discuss:
   - At what age they believe they knew the difference between right and wrong.
   - Who they think most influenced their attitudes to crime as a child.
   - Who they think their biggest influencers are now.

4. Invite feedback from each pair, ensuring that everyone knows that the age of criminal responsibility in England and Wales is 10 years old (8 to 12 in Scotland[1]). This means that children under this age cannot be arrested and charged with a crime, but there are other punishments that can be given to under-10s who break the law.

   Early influencers on attitudes to crime are likely to include parents/carers and other family members whilst friends and peers are likely to be more influential on young adults. Other influences (positive and negative) could include faith, community, media and popular culture.

5. Conclude by reminding the young people that although the views and opinions of others may influence their attitudes and values, when it comes to actions they alone are responsible. Suggest that if they are ever in a situation where they are unsure if something is the right thing to do, they wait until they have all the information and have considered all the potential consequences before making a decision. Doing so can help avoid doing something they may later regret.

---

1   See Age of Criminal Responsibility (Scotland) Act 2019: https://www.legislation.gov.uk/asp/2019/7/section/1/enacted

ATTITUDES TO CRIME

Please look at the list below and tick the box that corresponds best with your opinion:

		Yes, definitely a crime	Not really a crime	No, not a crime
1	Standing up for what you believe in			
2	Publicly disagreeing with the views of others			
3	Asking people to sign an online petition for a cause you believe in			
4	Making violent threats on social media to someone whose views you find offensive			
5	Being proud of where you come from			
6	Defending your family from criticism			
7	Believing that your ethnic heritage makes you superior to others			
8	Shouting abuse at someone in the street			
9	Not getting involved if you see bullying			
10	Defending your friends if they are in trouble			
11	Withholding information about a crime from the police			
12	Giving false information to the police			
13	Fighting back if someone physically assaults you			
14	Carrying a knife in self-defence			
15	Buying a replica weapon online			
16	Looking after drugs money for a friend			
17	Accepting money you know is from the proceeds of crime			
18	Threatening someone who owes you money			
19	Providing a partner with a false alibi			
20	Falsely accusing someone to get out of trouble			

ACTIVITY 15: EVIDENCE BAGS

Aims

- To investigate an imaginary crime using a set of props.
- To consider the crime that has been committed from the viewpoints of the perpetrator of the crime and the victim.
- To explore the ethos of UK justice.
- To signpost to sources of support for anyone who is a victim of crime.

Time: 90 minutes

Key vocabulary

- Crime and evidence
- Victim
- Perpetrator
- Justice

You will need

- 6 opaque plastic bags (e.g. bin liners, nappy sacks etc.)
- Copies of the Evidence Label
- Sticky tape
- Props to use as imaginary 'crime scene' evidence such as a toy gun, an empty wallet, a credit card, a bottle or a length of rope
- A small notebook and pencil for each group
- Paper and pens
- Copies of the Headlines: We Want Justice worksheet
- Information about Victim Support[2]

Facilitator note: Prepare for the activity by dividing the 'evidence' between the six bags and sealing them so that the props cannot be seen. Then complete an Evidence Label and stick it on the front of the sealed bag.

How to do it

1. Split the young people into six small groups and explain that for the purposes of this activity a gang-related crime has been committed and their job as 'detective' is to investigate and then devise a short piece of drama to explain what happened. They will be provided with a selection of props to use as a plot device.

2. Tell them that evidence has been found at the scene of each crime, which has been put into the 'evidence bags'. Explain that no other 'evidence' can be added to this. Invite a volunteer from each group to choose a bag to investigate, giving them a notebook and pencil to make notes in. They are now equipped to plan a scene that explains:
   - the crime that has been committed

---

2   www.victimsupport.org.uk

- the identity of the perpetrator(s) and their motivation for the crime
- the impact the crime has (or is likely to have) on the victim(s).

3. Allow 30 minutes to prepare and rehearse the scenario. The notebook and pencil can be used for note taking or to write a script. It is also permissible to use them as props within the scene.

4. Invite each group to perform their scenario. Lead a round of applause after each performance and then invite the audience to suggest what they think should happen if those committing the crime are caught. Record these decisions to reflect on later.

5. Once all of the performances have been given, review the crimes committed and the punishments suggested as a consequence of breaking the law. Ask:

- Comparing the crimes on a scale of causing the most to least harm, are the punishments fair?
- How might victims feel if these were the penalties given?
- Has 'justice' been done?

Suggest that one of the main aims of the legal justice system in the UK is that justice should be swift and fitting of the crime committed, and that it is important that both the victims and perpetrators of crime believe this to be so.

6. Divide the young people into pairs, giving each pair a copy of the Headlines: We Want Justice worksheet. These report on violent youth crimes in recent years that have resulted in serious injury. In some cases these are life changing, for example, acid attacks to the face, hands chopped off by machetes, internal organs damaged by knives and gun shot wounds. Explain that some parents and families believe that there is not enough support given to the victims of violence and their families.

Ask: What sort of support might a victim need? What type of support should be available for families?

7. Discuss ideas explaining that violent crime doesn't just cause physical damage; it can also negatively impact on mental health, both at the time and in the future. Inform young people about Victim Support,[3] an organization offering free, confidential help and support to any victim of crime in England and Wales.

8. Finally, explain that whilst some young people think gang membership offers things like respect, a sense of belonging etc. that build confidence and self-esteem, statistically young people in the criminal justice system are three times more likely to have mental health problems compared with their peers.[4] These include things like anxiety, depression and drug and alcohol dependence. Some of this can be due to early childhood trauma, including abuse and neglect, but it can also be due to their experiences within gang life, for example, sexual or criminal exploitation. Alongside this is the increased likelihood of being exposed to traumatic events, including witnessing or being a victim of violence.

---

3   In Scotland this service is provided by Victim Support Scotland (https://victimsupport.scot). In Northern Ireland those affected by crime can contact Victim Support NI (www.victimsupportni.com).
4   www.mentalhealth.org.uk/publications/mental-health-needs-young-offenders-update

EVIDENCE

Agency: . . . .

Item no: . . . .

Case no: . . . .

Date of collection: . . . .

Time of collection: . . . .

Collected by: . . . .

Description of evidence: . . . .

. . . .

. . . .

Location of collection: . . . .

. . . .

. . . .

Type of offence: . . . .

. . . .

Victim: . . . .

Subject: . . . .

Terror gang teenagers are tamed

She died in mum's arms

Drill, the 'demonic' music linked to rise in youth murders

'Drill music': a nihilistic genre filled with boasts of death and violence

Disturbing new form of British rap called Drill is blamed for surge in gang killings

Police targeting drill music videos in controversial crackdown on social media that 'incites violence'

ACTIVITY 16: TRIAGE ROOM

Aims

- To debate the ethics of treatment in an A&E department and who should take priority.
- To introduce the concept of taking personal responsibility for your actions.

Time: 45 minutes

Key vocabulary

- Victim
- Perpetrator
- Personal responsibility
- Health

You will need

- A copy of the Triage Room cards for each group of four

How to do it

1. At the weekend NHS hospital emergency (A&E) departments can be stretched to capacity with people presenting with everything from minor accidents to life-threatening injuries.

   > The NHS provides a comprehensive service, available to all irrespective of gender, race, disability, age, sexual orientation, religion or belief. It has a duty to each and every individual that it serves and must respect their human rights.[5]

   However, with limited resources, choices have to be made about the order in which patients are treated by a doctor unless it is a life or death situation or other extenuating circumstance. This decision-making process often starts with nurses, who assess patients in a triage room on arrival at the hospital.

   Explain that for this activity, everyone is going to be given the opportunity to be a triage nurse at an imaginary busy hospital and to make decisions about who should be treated first.

2. Divide the young people into groups of four and read the following scenario, which sets the scene:

   > It is midnight on a busy Friday night and you are a nurse in City Hospital Emergency Department. Two key members of staff called in sick, so everyone is having to work extra hard and do their best to cover the gap.
   >
   > Thankfully you only have an hour left of your shift and you can't wait to go home. So far tonight you have been threatened, spat at, vomited on and have endured lots of verbal abuse. You love your job but sometimes you wonder why you do it. All of the patients are in need of care, some are under the influence of alcohol or drugs, no one wants to wait, and everyone thinks that they should be seen first.

3. Give each group a set of the Triage Room cards. Explain, that on each of the cards is a summary of a patient waiting to be seen. The group task is to agree a system for prioritizing the order

---

5   NHS Constitution for England (www.gov.uk/government/publications/the-nhs-constitution-for-england).

patients are seen in and then use this to rank the cards. This should be a clear protocol that will be easily understood by patients should they challenge a nurse's decision.

Make the following points:

- Anything that could be used to damage another person, or threaten such actions, is classed as an offensive weapon. This could include things like hammers, corkscrews or even compasses.

- Carrying a knife significantly increases your chances of getting stabbed yourself.

- There is no 'safe place' to stab someone. A wound in the arm or leg can still kill someone if an artery is severed.

- If stabbed in the heart a person can 'bleed out' and die in less than a minute.

4. Allow up to 20 minutes for discussion and then invite each group to feedback their top priorities and to explain why. Go on to compare and contrast those cards rated lower and the reasons why.

Use some of these prompt questions to facilitate further discussion:

- Are some patients more deserving than others? How or why?

- Should patients who abuse or threaten staff be refused treatment? Why or why not?

- How much do people have a responsibility for maintaining their own health and wellbeing?

- Should those with injuries sustained through criminal activity have the same priority as those hurt through no fault of their own? Why or why not?

- Should people hurt through their own lifestyle choices have to pay for healthcare? Why or why not?

5. Conclude by explaining that all hospitals have a patient charter, which is usually displayed in public areas, setting out their ethos for providing healthcare, free at the point of access, to all.

TRIAGE ROOM

A 70-year-old woman who has broken her nose in a fall	A six-month-old baby with a high temperature
A 28-year-old drug dealer stabbed in the leg by a rival	A 19-year-old trans woman with face and chest burns from an acid attack
An 18-year-old man accidentally shot in the eye with a friend's BB gun	A 30-year-old man complaining of severe chest pains after using cocaine
A 40-year-old pregnant woman with whiplash injuries following a car accident	A 13-year-old boy with a broken leg from playing football
A 17-year-old boy injured with his own knife during a fight	A 15-year-old young woman injured and arrested during a gang fight
A 19-year-old student collapsed from alcohol poisoning	A 50-year-old man with hands burnt using firelighters to start a BBQ
A 60-year-old male with head injuries from a racist attack	

ACTIVITY 17: **REDUCING THE RISK**

Aims

- To identify potential community risks.
- To use problem-solving skills to reduce identified risks to acceptable levels.

Time: 60 minutes

Key vocabulary

- Assessing risks
- Confidence
- Making informed decisions

You will need

- Social Risk cards
- Flipchart paper or a whiteboard
- Red, orange and green colour marker pens

How to do it

1. Working in small groups, ask the young people to come up with their own definition of what is meant by a 'social situation' and then to make a list of potential social situations the young people may be in.

   Social situations could include: online and offline meet-ups, organized parties or impromptu gatherings, family or community celebrations, youth clubs, sports events or visiting the home of a friend.

2. Next, instruct them to review each situation to consider any potential risks they can identify:

   - to themselves
   - to others.

   Risks identified could include: drinking alcohol, using drugs, anti-social behaviour, unplanned or unprotected sex, smoking, food poisoning, walking home alone, dares, starting or getting into arguments, fighting, bullying, sexual assault, getting separated from friends or losing money or a phone.

3. Call the group back together and take suggestions from each group, recording them on flipchart paper or a whiteboard. Point out that in some of the places people socialize and/or congregate (e.g. public buildings like schools, libraries and theatres) there is health and safety legislation to help keep them safe, but in other contexts you have to do that for yourself. Whilst it's impossible to foresee every difficulty, it's important to build the skills, knowledge and confidence to be able to make informed decisions.

4. Give each small group a sheet of flipchart paper, coloured pens and a set of Social Risk cards. Ask for a volunteer from each group to draw a large set of traffic lights – red, orange (amber) and green. Explain that the Social Risk cards outline different situations that might arise when socializing with peers. Explain the traffic light system:

   - Red – unsafe
   - Amber – potential for risk, think first
   - Green – safer.

5. Task each group with discussing the cards and then placing them on the traffic lights to reflect the level of risk posed. Once done, review the task, encouraging suggestions as to how each risk can be reduced to an acceptable level.

Example: Amber: Being with friends who are known drug users. Ways to reduce risk:

-   Identify times when you know they will be more likely to take drugs and avoid making plans then.

-   Make it clear that you do not take drugs.

-   Do not offer to carry, buy or hide drugs, whatever the incentive.

-   Choose not to be with them when they have used drugs.

-   Leave if drugs are about to be used.

-   Get medical help if someone overdoses or becomes unwell.

-   Offer support if they decide to stop using drugs.

Encourage discussion using these prompt questions:

-   Is it possible to remove all risks from your life? *For example, suggest that everything in life has a risk attached to it but some risks are unacceptably high and are more likely to have negative consequences. Ultimately, trust your instincts – if you don't feel safe, leave.*

-   Are some risks worth taking? *For example, you may decide that high heels look great so are worth the risk of painful feet, but getting into a car when you don't know the driver isn't.*

-   When does a risk become too high? *For example, when the likelihood of a negative outcome becomes probable; when the consequences are likely to cause serious harm or even death; when the odds are against a positive result etc.*

Point out that it isn't only young people who take risks; everyone, regardless of their age, should consider personal safety a priority.

SOCIAL RISK

Sitting in an empty train carriage	Taking a short cut through an unlit area	Booking a taxi home
Eating food from a takeaway van	Stepping in to try to stop a fight	Carrying money, cards and a phone
Getting a pizza delivered	Defending a friend in an argument	Meeting up in a derelict building
Sharing personal information with new acquaintances	Carrying a knife for personal protection	Being with friends who are known drug users
Taking on dares to impress your friends	Talking to peers you don't know	Sharing online pornography via social media
Drinking alcohol out in the community	Asking strangers for cigarettes	Getting into conversation with unknown adults
Asking adults to buy alcohol to drink	Meeting up with friends outside in the community	Leaving a drunk friend to get home on their own
Accepting a lift from someone you just met	Wearing high heels you can't walk properly in	Using fake ID to get into a club
Carrying a condom in your wallet/purse	Agreeing to carry drugs for someone else	Carrying your phone in your back pocket
Picking up discarded syringe needles	Witnessing a crime	Challenging extreme views expressed by others
Getting on the back of a moped	Going to the house of a known offender	Playing drinking games with shots
Walking through an area known for gangs	Telling people how much cash you have	Going out without a coat in winter
Riding a bike on the pavement	Going out without any money	Playing football in the street

ACTIVITY 18: PERCEPTIONS AND REALITIES

Aims

- To explore feelings about the perceptions and realities of street crime.
- To consider practical ways to reduce risks in the community.

Time: 30–45 minutes

Key vocabulary

- Gang
- Community safety
- Crime

You will need

- Masking tape
- 2 sheets of A4 paper marked 'Safe' and 'Extremely unsafe'
- Sticky notes and pens
- Copies of the Perceptions and Realities Scenario

How to do it

1. Lay masking tape on the floor (or the wall) in a straight line. Stick the 'Safe' and 'Extremely unsafe' signs at each end of this continuum.

2. Give each person 6–8 sticky notes and a pen. Explain that you are going to read out a short scenario and as you do, the young people should jot down the feelings and emotions they think the character, 'Sarah', will experience, and stick them on the continuum between the two poles 'Safe' and 'Extremely unsafe'. To try to make this as close to 'real time' as possible, the sticky notes can be stuck onto the masking tape line as you go along.

   At this point there is no need to share what has prompted the feelings, as these will be considered later on, when the scenario is complete.

3. Review the feelings captured on the masking tape continuum, which are likely to range from happy at the start (i.e., Safe) through to anxious and concerned to scared and threatened (i.e., Extremely unsafe) and back to the 'Safe' end of the scale when Sarah realizes that there is nothing to worry about. Ask:

   - What was Sarah worried about? *For example, being mugged, assaulted or raped.*

   - What do you think her fears were based on? *For example, stereotypes about groups of young men wearing 'hoodies'; media coverage of gang-related crime; previous experiences of young men etc.*

   - Why do you think she reminded herself of her own experiences as a teenager? *For example, to try to put what was happening into perspective; to remind herself that not all young people dressed in hoodies are out to make trouble; to comfort herself with memories of times that she has managed challenging situations well; to help her keep calm.*

   All of these factors led Sarah to believe that she was at risk of attack from a gang of youths. These assumptions increased her fear and anxiety, even though she tried hard to rationalize the situation by drawing on her own experiences.

In reality the young men may or may not have been members of a gang. Their change in behaviour was due to the arrival of the young women and had nothing to do with Sarah and her lone journey home. Her perception of crime impacted on her assessment of the situation.

4. Discuss whether walking past a group like the one in the scenario is a risk, and if so, whether some sectors of the community are more at risk than others. Take the opportunity to explore perceptions of crime and make the point that although Sarah as a 42-year-old woman walking home alone at night may feel at high risk and is right to be cautious, statistically there is a greater likelihood of young men (aged 16–24) being a victim of violent crime.[6]

    According to the 2018 Crime Survey of England and Wales (CSEW):[7]

    –   More people worry that they will be a victim of crime than actually experience it.

    –   Older people report feeling vulnerable to crime but in reality young men in areas of higher deprivation are the most likely to become victims.

    –   Younger people spend more time out at night and are more likely to come into contact with people who become violent after consuming alcohol.

    –   16- to 24-year-olds from White, Black and Mixed ethnic groups are more likely to experience crime than people in the same age group from Asian and Other ethnic groups.

5. Move on to discuss strategies for keeping safe in the community, suggesting that we all have a responsibility to try to keep ourselves safe and to report anything we see that might put others in danger. Suggestions could include:

    –   always telling a parent/carer where you are going

    –   planning how to get home in advance

    –   walking with friends

    –   avoiding unlit areas after dark

    –   keeping a phone charged but out of sight (e.g. in a pocket)

    –   avoiding direct confrontations or not starting arguments

    –   making safe choices about alcohol and drugs

    –   reporting concerns to the police or Crimestoppers (this can be done anonymously).

---

6   'The nature of violent crime in England and Wales: year ending March 2018.' Available at www.ons.gov.uk/peoplepopulationandcommunity/crimeandjustice/articles/thenatureofviolentcrimeinenglandandwales/yearendingmarch2018

7   'Crime in England and Wales: Annual trend and demographic tables.' Available at www.ons.gov.uk/peoplepopulationandcommunity/crimeandjustice/datasets/crimeinenglandandwalesannualtrendanddemographictables

PERCEPTIONS AND REALITIES SCENARIO

Sarah is a 42-year-old woman. She works in the town council offices and is walking home after an evening out with work friends at a local pizza restaurant. She has had a really good time and is feeling relaxed and happy. Glancing up at the clock on the church she notices it's 22.30, much later than she thought.

Crossing the empty street her attention is caught by a group of young men gathered in the doorway of a shop. Dressed in dark hoodies and jeans, with baseball caps pulled low over their faces, the occasional flash of white from their trainers is caught in the streetlights as they talk and laugh loudly together.

Suddenly the boys stop talking and seem to be looking straight at her. Sarah hears a loud shout followed by other loud male voices. Instinctively she holds her handbag tighter, this could be a gang and she worries she could be mugged or worse. She quickly looks around to see if there is a way to continue without walking past them.

'Calm down', she tells herself, 'you were a teenager yourself once and you know how boisterous young men can be. They are probably harmless.'

Without warning other memories slide into her head too, horrible memories of being mocked and bullied by boys at school. Her teenage years had not been good ones. Panic starts to rise as the young men walk towards her.

Just as she decides to turn around and run back the way she came, Sarah sees two young women appear out of the shadows. She hears them greet the boys and immediately realizes that the young men were shouting to the girls, trying to get their attention.

Relief floods through her. 'False alarm', she thinks, and walks on home.

ACTIVITY 19: STOP AND SEARCH

Aims

- To check out knowledge and challenge any misconceptions about stop and search laws.
- To inform young people of their rights and what to do in the event of being stopped by police.

Time: 30 minutes

Key vocabulary

- Stop and search
- Police and the law

You will need

- 2 sheets of A4 paper marked 'True' and 'False'
- Flipchart paper and marker pens

How to do it

1. Prepare the room in advance for this activity by placing the 'True' and 'False' sheets of paper at opposite sides of the room.

   Ask: What would you like to happen if the police think a crime is about to happen in your area? Invite the young people to call out ideas and record them on the flipchart paper to refer back to later. These could include things like 'stop the crime' to more specific suggestions informed by current knowledge of the criminal justice system like 'arrest', 'detain' or 'restrain'.

   Ask: What powers do the police have if they see someone they think might commit a crime? Again, ask for suggestions and write them down.

2. Inform the young people that in the UK the police have the power to stop and question you at any time and if appropriate, stop and search. The point of these powers is to try to keep neighbourhoods as safe as possible. Questions that are likely to be asked include your name, your address and what you are planning to do. Ask for a show of hands to find out if young people think this is acceptable to them and if so why or why not.

3. Explain that you are going to facilitate a quiz to find out how much everyone knows about 'stop and search' powers. Make it clear that the aim of the quiz is to learn, so it doesn't matter if there are different levels of knowledge within the group.

4. Read out the quiz questions in turn and then ask the young people to move to the 'True' or 'False' point in the room as appropriate.

5. After each round give the correct answer and use the information given with it to prompt a short discussion.

Additional information:

- The main legislation that covers stop and search is the Police and Criminal Evidence Act. Searches for controlled drugs are covered by the Misuse of Drugs Act 1971.

- The Stop and Search Code of Practice sets out what the police should do when stopping and searching. This includes treating people fairly and with respect, and carrying out a search in a reasonable time.

- If nothing is found, the individual is free to go. The police officer will give a receipt, which is a record of the search. A copy of this is available anytime within 12 months of the search.

- If an under-18 is taken for a more thorough search, a responsible adult will be present. This could be a parent or family member, foster carer or social worker depending on the situation and who has parental responsibility.[8]

---

8   'Police powers to stop and search: your rights.' Available at www.gov.uk/police-powers-to-stop-and-search-your-rights

STOP AND SEARCH QUIZ

1. A police officer has the power to stop and search anyone at any time.

   False: The police have the power to stop and search if they have reasonable grounds to believe that someone has been involved in a crime or is in possession of a prohibited item. This includes:

   - illegal drugs
   - a weapon
   - stolen property
   - something that could be used to commit a crime, for example, a crowbar.

   The only exception for being stopped and searched without reasonable grounds is if it has been approved by a senior police officer on suspicion that a serious crime has been or is about to be committed.

2. If you refuse to stop or be searched the Human Rights Act says the police can't do anything about it.

   False: If someone refuses to be stopped, the police can use reasonable force to stop and detain so they can do a search; best advice is to comply.

3. A police officer or a police community support officer (PCSO) can stop and ask where you're going instead of carrying out a search.

   True: This is known as 'stop and account'. Legally you don't have to stop or answer any questions and refusal is not grounds for arrest.

4. Stop and search is the same as being arrested.

   False: An arrest may follow stop and search, depending on what the police find.

5. Before you can be searched a police officer must tell you the reasons why they have stopped you.

   True: You must also be told:

   - the name, ID number and police station of the officer
   - what they expect to find, for example, illegal drugs
   - why the search is legal
   - how to get a record or copy of the search.[9]

6. A police officer can demand you strip to your underwear in a public place if they are searching you.

   False: A police officer can ask you to take off your coat, jacket or gloves and also ask to see the contents of your pockets or a bag. If they require a 'more thorough search' and ask you to remove other clothes or something worn for religious or cultural reasons (e.g. a hijab or turban), an officer who identifies as the same gender must take you somewhere out of public view.

7. Stop and searches can be carried out on children.

   True: There is no age limit for stop and search, but police guidance says: 'It is important for the officer to remember that a child should be treated as a child first and foremost, even if they are known to the police or appear older. If that child or young person is putting themselves in a situation where they may be at risk of harm, then that should be the officer's priority.'[10]

---

9   'Police powers to stop and search: your rights.' Available at www.gov.uk/police-powers-to-stop-and-search-your-rights

10   College of Policing (2016) Authorised Professional Practice, 'Stop and Search – Professional.' London: College of Policing, para. 2.3.2. Available at www.app.college.police.uk/app-content/stop-and-search/professional/#children

8. Parents and/or carers must be informed if a child has been stopped and searched.

   False: A record of the search will be given to the young person but the police are not required to inform parents or carers that a search of their child has taken place, unless they have any safety concerns.

9. Black working-class young men are far more likely than their white peers to be stopped and searched.

   Debatable: No one should be stopped and searched because of their race, age, gender, sexual orientation, disability, religion or faith or because they are 'known to the police' or have committed a crime in the past. However, 2017 statistics reveal that white offenders have the highest conviction rate[11] but young black men are more likely to be stopped and searched.

10. If you get stopped and searched you can't complain; it's just how it is.

    False: If you believe you have been stopped and searched unreasonably, not treated fairly or with respect, a complaint can be made to:

    - local police station
    - Citizens Advice Bureau[12]
    - Independent Police Complaints Commission[13]
    - Equality and Human Rights Commission[14]
    - solicitor.

---

11 Ministry of Justice (2016) 'Statistics on Race and the Criminal Justice System 2016.' Available at https://assets.publishing.service.gov.uk/government/uploads/system/uploads/attachment_data/file/663376/race-cjs-2016-infographic.pdf

12 www.citizensadvice.org.uk

13 The Independent Office for Police Conduct replaced the Independent Police Complaints Commission in 2018; see www.policeconduct.gov.uk

14 www.equalityhumanrights.com/en

ACTIVITY 20: CRIME AND PUNISHMENT

Aims

- To explore different attitudes to crime and punishment.

- To begin to understand how personal values can impact on perceptions of right and wrong.

Time: 45 minutes

Key vocabulary

- Attitudes

- Values

- Crime and punishment

You will need

- Sets of the Crime cards (one set per group of four)

How to do it

1. Start by asking the following question: When it comes to justice, do you think the punishment should fit the crime?

2. Invite the young people to discuss in small groups what they think this means and then decide if they agree or disagree with it as a principle for justice and why. Allow up to 10 minutes for discussion and then invite feedback of key points, encouraging debate where there is a difference of opinion.

   Use the following prompt questions to explore further:

   - If a crime is committed, should someone 'pay' for it?

   - Can a punishment ever be proportionate to the crime?

   - If all punishments were the same, would there be more or less incentive to commit crime?

3. Suggest that the answers to these questions are likely to work from the starting point that some crimes are more serious than others. Explain that the next part of this session is going to explore personal opinions on this.

4. Give each group a set of Crime cards. Their task is to discuss the crime outlined on each and then rate the cards in order of severity, with what they consider to be the most serious at the top and the least serious at the bottom.

5. Allow up to 15 minutes discussion time and then ask each group to feedback their Crime cards in order. Again, pick out any differences or unusual responses for discussion and then review how decisions were made.

   Use the following prompt questions to explore different viewpoints:

   - Is there such a thing as a 'victimless crime'? If so, how and which? *Consider the wider implications of crimes that at first glance may appear to harm no one, for example, shoplifting may be covered by commercial insurance but ultimately theft could lead to higher premiums that companies will need to make back by raising prices for customers etc.*

   - Is it morally worse to commit a crime against someone you know? *Consider things like breaking trust, betrayal and the emotional impact of offending against someone you know.*

- Do some crimes impact on the wider community? *Consider things like areas becoming 'known' for crime, people feeling unsafe, stirring up of tensions between different groups etc.*

6. Conclude that in the UK, which is a democratic society, justice means that laws apply equally to all and that everyone has the right to a fair trial. These principles have been developed by courts over centuries and include the assumption of innocence until proven guilty, the right to be represented and to a fair and public hearing.

CRIME

Shoplifting	'Borrowing' money without asking from friends/family
Borrowing money from an unlicensed source	Making contactless payments with a stolen bank card
Applying for credit using stolen personal data	Making a false insurance claim
Accepting money for giving false information	Pick pocketing
Making a fraudulent benefit claim	Tax evasion
Selling counterfeit (fake) goods online	Blackmail
Street robbery	Trespass
Robbing a house	Causing actual bodily harm

ACTIVITY 21: COURT STATEMENTS

Aims

- To understand the term 'mitigating factor'.
- To explore examples of common mitigating factors.
- To discuss different viewpoints about how and when mitigating factors should affect the legal consequences of breaking the law.

Time: 60 minutes

Key vocabulary

- Gang-related crime
- Court
- Gender
- Legal consequences

You will need

- Flipchart paper and marker pens
- Copies of the Court Statements

How to do it

1. Divide the young people into small groups and give out flipchart paper and marker pens.

2. Read out the following 'Arrest scenario' to set the scene. Write tasks 'a' and 'b' on a large sheet of paper and display it where everyone can see.

Arrest scenario

A young person has been arrested in connection with gang-related crime, which they admit to. They are charged with assault and intimidation and have been bailed to appear in court in two weeks time.

You will shortly be given an extract from the police statement that they made. The young person says it explains how they got involved in the gang and why they commit crime. They are asking for this to be taken into account in court.

In UK criminal law these explanations about the circumstances of a crime, along with any personal details that could impact on the crime, for example peer pressure, criminal exploitation or coercion, are called 'mitigating factors'. These will be presented to the court and might result in reduced charges or a lesser sentence.

Your task is to read the statement and assess:

- how much you think it explains their choices and why

- if you think it should influence any sentence or fine they receive.

---

3. Give each group a copy of the Court Statements to study. They should discuss and make notes under the headings 'Reasons for' and 'Reasons against' before deciding if they think the application to have this submitted to the court should be upheld or if they think it should be denied.

4. Allow 20 minutes for discussion and then bring everyone back together. Invite each group in turn to read out their statement and then present their findings, ending with a decision to deny or uphold the request.

5. Once everyone has presented and time has been allowed for questions, share the following:

The Sentencing Council of England and Wales[15] lists the following as possible mitigating factors:

Factors indicating lower culpability:

- a greater degree of provocation than normally expected

- mental illness or disability

- youth or age, where it affects the responsibility of the individual defendant

- the fact that the offender played only a minor role in the offence.

Offender mitigation:

- genuine remorse

- admissions to police in interview

- ready cooperation with authorities.

Self-defence is *not* a mitigating factor.

6. Then ask each group to indicate if they assumed a male or female offender made the request for mitigating factors to be considered. Point out that all of the names assigned to the statements are gender-neutral. Ask:

- What led you to assume the person making the statement was male or female?

- What assumptions did you make because of this?

- How did it impact on your discussions?

- Would this have been different had you known the gender? Why or why not?

7. Conclude that although far more young men than women are reported to be in a gang, women and girls can be linked to gang-related criminal activity. In addition to all-female gangs, research suggests that young women and girls often enter gang life whilst still at school and are likely to be introduced by boyfriends who are already involved. According to Home Office[16] reports, their role within the gang is not just as perpetrators of crime but also as victims:

- carrying or storing weapons and/or drugs, as young men are more likely to be searched

- committing or inciting violence

- sexual exploitation and as victims of physical and sexual violence.

Explain that the criminal justice system makes the following provision for young people:[17]

- Youth courts in England and Wales are held in magistrates' court buildings. Some have a separate youth courtroom.

- Youth courts are not open to the public.

- Before going to court a Youth Offending Team (YOT) worker will be allocated and a pre-sentence report written. This will take into account information from parents/carers, schools and other professionals working with the young person and their family as well as the young person themselves.

---

15 www.sentencingcouncil.org.uk/explanatory-material/magistrates-court/item/aggravating-and-mitigating-factors
16 https://assets.publishing.service.gov.uk/government/uploads/system/uploads/attachment_data/file/491802/horr88.pdf, p.50.
17 Please note that this differs in Scotland and other nations that have a separate criminal justice system. Please check what is applicable where you are.

- Cases are heard by three magistrates or a single district judge sitting alone.

- No one wears a wig or a formal gown, and young people are referred to by their first name.

- Only the most serious crimes, for example, murder, rape, terrorism or serious firearms charges, are heard in Crown Court. This is where the likelihood of a custodial sentence is greater.

- If a child has been given a detention and training order of six months or less it becomes 'spent' 18 months after the sentence is completed. If their sentence was for more than six months, it will take two years. Some of the most serious convictions, such as rape and murder, remain on record and a child offender will have to continue declaring it to future employers for the rest of their lives.[18]

---

18   For more information about the youth justice system in England and Wales, go to www.cps.gov.uk/youth-crime

COURT STATEMENTS

Statement 1: 'I didn't fit in so got in with a group of known troublemakers for protection, to become someone who wasn't a victim of homophobic bullying any longer.' (Sam, age 17)

Statement 2: 'It was expected of me because of where I live. It made life easier just to conform to the stereotype.' (Jess, age 14)

Statement 3: 'My brother does it so everyone assumed I was a drug dealer too. In the end I thought I might as well make some money as I was accused anyway.' (Jet, age 19)

Statement 4: 'I got in with older boys from the estate, I liked the culture, the music, the money – then I found myself in something I couldn't get out of.' (Sasha, age 16)

Statement 5: 'Everyone looked to me to sort it out as I'm the tallest, and then I had a reputation to protect. I don't want to lose face but I wish things were different.' (Charley, age 15)

Statement 6: 'I was put in care when I was five and never saw my mum. I was lonely and being with a gang gave me a new family that cared for me.' (Nat, age 16)

ACTIVITY 22: GANG STEREOTYPES AND GENDER

Aims

- To differentiate between gender-based stereotypes and recorded evidence.
- To consider the different risks and vulnerabilities associated with gangs for young men and young women.
- To consider the potential consequences of gang membership.

Time: 2 hours

Key vocabulary

- Gangs
- Stereotypes
- Discrimination
- Gender
- Peer exploitation
- Consequences

You will need

- Flipchart paper and marker pens
- Facilities to show the Home Office infographic 'Statistics on Race and the Criminal Justice System, 2018'[19]
- Copies of the Court Statements
- Films: Channel 4 clip, 'Young Gang Members on What Makes a Real Man' taken from the Grayson Perry *All Man* series[20] and the BBC Three documentary *Britain's Toughest Girl Gangs* (13.01 minutes)[21]

How to do it

1. Divide the young people into small groups and task them with drawing a 'typical' young person who belongs to a gang. Only allow 5 minutes for the task and encourage them to go with their first ideas. The drawing can be labelled to draw attention to key features that identify this person as a member of a gang. This could include:

   - where they live
   - what they wear
   - how they look
   - what their home life is like
   - what they do
   - who they are likely to be with.

---

19 Available at https://assets.publishing.service.gov.uk/government/uploads/system/uploads/attachment_data/file/849201/race-cjs-2018-infographic.pdf
20 www.youtube.com/watch?v=VB0EqEnadOc
21 www.youtube.com/watch?v=xHKccU2NYDQ

2. Call time and without sharing what has been drawn ask the following questions, asking a representative from each group to raise a hand if this is something they have drawn or written:

   – How many drew a young man?

   – How many drew the gang member wearing a hoodie?

   – How many drew or wrote something related to alcohol or drugs?

   – How many thought they were likely to live in social housing or in a deprived area?

   – How many thought they were unlikely to be in education, training or employment?

3. Now invite them to share their pictures with their nearest group and to look at similarities and differences. It is likely that in addition to the stereotypes outlined above others, including ethnicity, will be highlighted.

   Suggest that stereotypes like this are unhelpful, as they don't show the full picture and can lead to prejudice and discrimination against some groups.

4. Show the Home Office infographic, and then compare and contrast this with their earlier drawings. Ask:

   – Were you surprised by any of the statistics in the infographic? Why or why not?

   – Has it changed any of the assumptions you made?[22]

5. Move on to explore gender stereotypes and discriminatory attitudes and how this impacts on peer pressure to conform to gang culture. Divide the young people into small groups and give them a large sheet of paper and a pen for each person. Show the Grayson Perry clip. Part of a series, Grayson Perry explores contemporary masculinity, visiting ultra-male worlds to explore the changing lives and expectations of men in Britain today.

   Whilst it is playing, ask the young people to notice and make notes on:

   – what they say about gang membership and the culture they share

   – any gender stereotypes identified

   – discriminatory attitudes to others expressed by the young men.

6. When it has finished, invite each group to share their findings, encouraging them to identify any stereotypes and how their discriminatory attitudes, for example, to those living in another town, might lead to gang clashes or anti-social behaviour.

7. Show the BBC Three documentary made in 2017, *Britain's Toughest Girl Gangs*.

Facilitator note: Please be aware that the young women in this film talk about sexual exploitation and it contains frank and graphic conversations, so please check that it is appropriate for your group.

8. Afterwards facilitate a whole group discussion that asks:

   – Do you think the documentary is representative of 'girl gangs'? Why or why not?

   – How are they different to the way young men in gangs are portrayed?

   – The documentary says that loneliness is a big factor in the choice to join a gang. Why do you think this is?

   – Do you see the young women as victims or perpetrators? Why?

   – What else could be done to support these young women and discourage others from making similar choices?

---

22 For the whole report, see https://assets.publishing.service.gov.uk/government/uploads/system/uploads/attachment_data/file/849200/statistics-on-race-and-the-cjs-2018.pdf

ACTIVITY 23: VIOLENCE IN GAMING

Aims

- To explore the impact that watching different genres of media has on feelings, emotions and mood.
- To research the effect that watching violent games can have on attitudes to aggressive behaviour and violence.
- To consider if exposure to high-resolution images of weapons and extreme violence can impact on real-world actions.

Time: 60 minutes

Key vocabulary

- Video games
- Gaming
- Attitudes to violence
- Weapons

You will need

- Internet access and a large enough screen for showing extracts of films to the group
- A selection of memes or short film clips of animals doing something super cute or amusing (Instagram, YouTube or TikTok are great for these)
- The opening sequences of video games that contain violence and weapons, for example, Fortnite, Grand Theft Auto, Doom, Call of Duty, Mortal Kombat (these can be found on YouTube)
- 4 sheets of paper headed 'Not at all', 'Some', 'A bit' and 'A lot', extra paper and pens
- 3 sheets of flipchart paper, marker pens and sticky tack
- A copy of the Four Zone Questions

Facilitator note: Prepare the room by displaying the four pre-prepared sheets of paper in the four corners of a room. These will be used in the second part of the session.

How to do it

1. Read out the following quote:

   What better way to stop knife crime than by stopping young people from picking up knives in the first place?[23]

   Facilitate a short discussion asking the young people if they agree with the statement and then asking them to suggest anything that they think influences decisions to carry a weapon. This could include:

   - fear
   - peer pressure
   - believing that 'everyone' does it

---

23 Former Home Secretary The Rt Hon Amber Rudd MP, Serious Violence Strategy, launched on 9 April 2018. Available at www.gov.uk/government/news/home-secretary-to-launch-serious-violence-strategy

- seeing weapons used on TV or in films

- music or music videos

- video games.

Explain that the use of firearms in the UK is tightly controlled by legislation, which is arguably why the UK has one of the lowest gun homicide rates in the world. It is also illegal to possess a knife (with a few exceptions). However, there is an ongoing debate about the impact that exposure to guns and weapons via violent video games has on young people, and whether it desensitizes them to real-life violence and/or increases the likelihood of engaging in violent behaviour. Explain that in this session you are going to explore both sides of this argument further.

2. Begin the session in a seated circle. Give each young person a piece of paper and a pen and ask everyone to write down one word to describe how they feel in that moment. In turn, invite them to read out their word and write it up on a large sheet of paper to create a 'wordstorm'. Take a marker pen and write the heading 'Baseline mood' at the top. Briefly comment on the diverse feelings, emotions and moods expressed within the group before sticking the wordstorm up on the wall.

3. Show the selection of cute animal film clips. At the end ask the young people to write down a couple of words or a short sentence to describe thoughts and feelings (a) when they watched them and (b) after watching them.

4. Create another wordstorm poster using feedback from the responses to watching the animal clips. This could include:

- feeling warm

- protective

- happy/smiley

- relaxed

- like you want to stroke/pet the animals

- like you want to cuddle the animals

- love and affection.

Head this poster 'The feel good factor' and stick it next to the previous one.

5. Move straight on to show the video game trailers, repeating the exercise straight afterwards to capture thoughts and feelings during and after watching virtual violence and aggression. Again, invite feedback and create another wordstorm poster from the young people's suggestions. These could include feeling:

- tense

- excited

- stimulated

- agitated

- 'pumped up'

- aggressive

- ready for action.

Ask the young people for suggestions about the title for this wordstorm poster.

6. Facilitate a review across the three freshly created wordstorms to see how exposure to the different types of virtual stimuli has impacted on feelings, thoughts and mood from the baseline devised at the start. Ask:

- If the purpose of the cute animal clips is to make people smile and feel good, what is the purpose of games containing graphic violence? *Suggest that some believe that over-exposure to violent video games negatively impacts on users because they become immune to the pain and suffering they see on screen.*

- What types of violence are shown in these games? *As well as discussing the different types of violence, including torture and death, ask the young people to comment on the potential impact of regularly seeing blood, guts and gore. Ask them to consider the role of women and minorities within well-known games to identify any differences in the types of violence inflicted on them. Consider how this might impact on real-life attitudes to diversity.*

- How does it feel as a player to be inflicting this level of harm on an 'enemy' or 'target'? *How does this fit with notions of loyalty, defending honour and fighting for a cause already discussed in the context of gangs?*

Explain that over the last 30 years, since the development of video games containing violence, there have been media headlines claiming that they are damaging. There has been research conducted but often this has later been proved flawed, limited or has dated very quickly, so the wider impact of video games on attitudes to violence, crime and carrying weapons is not known for certain. For example, the American Psychological Association (APA) Task Force says their studies:

> show a small but reliable and well-established causal link between violent video game exposure and aggressive behaviour, including 'insults, threats, hitting, pushing, hair pulling, biting and other forms of verbal and physical aggression'.[24]

7. Introduce the four zones in the room created earlier. Explain that you are going to read out a few questions and then ask them to move to the zone that best reflects their opinions. There are prompt points and arguments for and against underneath each question to help facilitators promote debate and discussion between rounds.

---

24   https://arstechnica.com/gaming/2020/03/apa-warns-against-linking-violent-video-games-to-real-world-violence

FOUR ZONE QUESTIONS

'Not at all', 'A bit', 'Quite a lot', 'A lot'

1. How much do you think computer game rating systems protect children from watching violent content?

    Rating systems classify violence, nudity and language in video games. They are there to protect children and under-18s, but the classification codes don't always stop them accessing violent games. However, not everyone adheres to this guidance, resulting in exposure at a younger age than recommended.

2. How important is realism to you in video game violence?

    Mention that Virtual Reality (VR) devices enable gamers to feel as though they are actually there. How ethical is this in the context of violent games? Is it a good or bad thing to experience inflicting extreme violence on others in realistic ways?

3. In your opinion, how much does exposure to online violence affect real-life attitudes?

    Explain that some experts believe that repeated exposure to violent video games contributes to some young people becoming violent or committing extreme anti-social behaviour. In many games, violence is rewarded with higher scores and higher status within the game. Does this send a message for real life?

4. Do you think the experience of choosing and carrying weapons in a video game can affect the choice to carry a weapon in real life?

    Some argue that the vast array of weapons shown in video games reinforces the idea that being armed protects you, encouraging people to want one. Can seeing something make you want to do it? Consider both sides of this argument, for example, there is evidence to prove that drug education doesn't make people want to take drugs but there is plenty of evidence to show that advertising a product on TV results in a sales boost.

5. Can video games that glorify war, gangs etc. be blamed for street violence?

    Some argue that repeatedly seeing kicking, stabbing, shooting etc. on screen reduces empathy in real-life situations by presenting maim and torture as 'justified' ways of resolving conflict. Others think that playing violent video games actually has the opposite effect; it gets aggression 'out of the system' so people are less likely to engage in it in the real world.

6. Do you think people are easily able to leave the emotional affects of interactive video games behind when the game ends?

    This includes things like increased levels of anxiety and fear during and after playing as well as any feelings of aggression. The World Health Organization (WHO) includes 'gaming disorder'[25] on its official list of mental health conditions, stating that gaming behaviour could qualify as problematic if it interferes significantly in other areas of people's lives.

7. Return to the original quote from Amber Rudd and ask: Do you think that tightening up laws around the levels of violence in video games would reduce the numbers of people 'picking up' a weapon? Conduct a quick poll using a show of hands and then discuss why or why not.

8. Conclude that video games offer players an opportunity to take on alternative identities and behave in ways that would never be acceptable in the real world.

    Whilst there is no hard indisputable evidence one way or the other that this is harmful, these games can be problematic for some players. Remind young people that in the real world we are all responsible for our own actions, and suggest that anyone concerned that gaming has become compulsive or is worried about their emotional, mental or physical health should ask for help and support. This could be via a GP or by talking to another trusted adult.

---

25   www.who.int/news-room/q-a-detail/gaming-disorder

Section Three

DECISION-MAKING

ACTIVITY 24: INFLUENCE AND PERSUASION

Aims

- To gain a wider understanding of the factors that influence decision-making.
- To identify examples of when young people were influenced when making a decision.
- To consider responsibilities for decisions made.

Time: 60 minutes

Key vocabulary

- Influence
- Persuasion
- Decision-making
- Responsibility

You will need

- Flipchart paper and marker pens
- Sticky notes and pens
- Decision cards (one set for every group of four, cut up and ready to use)
- Copies of the Influence and Persuasion Case Study

How to do it

1. Divide the young people into groups of four or five. Give each group 20 blank sticky notes and a pen.

2. Explain that they have 10 minutes to discuss and agree TWENTY decisions a person is likely to make in their life *before* the age of 25. Keep this activity fast-paced, so reduce the time if required. Ideas for decisions made could include:

   - what to spend pocket money on
   - which clothes to wear
   - what to eat (e.g. vegetarian, vegan etc.)
   - which music artists to follow
   - who to have as a friend
   - who to have a romantic relationship with
   - when to have sex/not to have sex
   - what to do after school/college/university
   - whether to learn to drive (or not)
   - who to vote for.

   Each idea should be written on a different sticky note. Call time and ask for examples but don't get into a conversation about why or how decisions are made, as this discussion comes next.

3. Introduce three types of decision-making:

   - **No decision**, where you let others decide what you are going to do

- **Snap decision**, where you decide quickly without thinking about the likely consequences, positive or negative

- **Responsible decision**, where you think through all the options, considering the impact your decision could have on yourself and others, before coming to a decision.

4. Give each group a copy of the Decision cards and task them with looking back through the decisions they identified and then discussing which type of decision-making style was (or will be) used.

5. Give out extra sticky notes and ask each group member to think about a decision they have made using each of the three types and why. For example:

   - Which primary school you went to = No decision, my parent(s) chose.

   - A new pair of trainers = Snap decision, I saw them and had to have them.

   - Which course I applied for at college = Responsible decision, I had my exam results, I know what area I want to work in, I looked at the college prospectus, I talked it over with a teacher, my best friend and my parent/carer, I went to visit the college and then I decided.

6. Invite feedback from each group as to how they ranked their original decisions and then ask them to share some of their own examples. Ask:

   - Does 'No decision' mean no responsibility for the outcomes? *If you never make any choices, does it mean you're not responsible for anything?*

   - Are 'Snap decisions' always bad? *Encourage examples where making a fast decision without much thought has resulted in a positive outcome, for example, saying 'yes' to an opportunity that has presented itself that has exceeded expectations. Then consider the downsides of making fast decisions, for example, not thinking through the negative consequences something might have on you or others.*

   - Which type of decision-making is most likely to end in a result you will remain happy with? *There are no guarantees, but if you have thought through a decision, considered both the potential for positive and negative outcomes and made a responsible decision, you are more likely to be content with the consequences.*

   - Which decisions are you more likely to be prepared to accept responsibility for? *Reflect back on some of the reasons identified for joining a gang, for example, emotional frustration, feeling that things are being 'done' without your say-so and believing that you have no way of getting your voice heard.*

7. Move on to look at external sources that can influence decisions. With the young people still in their groups, give out copies of the Influence and Persuasion Case Study. Ask them to read Part 1 and then discuss, considering the following questions, noting down their responses to feedback later:

   - Who is to blame for what has happened?

   - Is Abe a 'bad' person?

   - What influences might his home life have?

   - What responsibilities does Abe have for what happened?

8. Now give out Part 2 for them to read before considering these questions:

   - Is Abe's mum right to feel ashamed?

   - Do you think the type of music you listen to can influence your attitudes, values or behaviour?

   - What other factors might influence a decision? *For example, friends/peer pressure, wanting to conform, a lack of experience, state of mind, societal values, understanding of the situation and empathy for others etc.*

    – What can Abe do now? *Consider what reparation he can make to the young women, making the point that he can't make it right but he can perhaps make things better.*

Suggest that sometimes people get caught up in situations they know to be wrong but feel powerless to do anything. This does not mean that they are not responsible. Additional factors like drinking alcohol or drugs misuse can also impact on decisions that are later regretted.

9. Now ask each the group to discuss and then share an experience of being asked to do something they did not want to do. This doesn't have to be something major, for example, being asked to tidy their bedroom, get up to go to college/school or a friend asking them to do a favour.

   As each example is offered ask what the person did to try to persuade them. Examples could include:

   – emotional blackmail

   – bribery

   – telling them they will be in trouble if they don't

   – offering a reward

   – threatening them with something

   – offering them support to complete the task.

10. Write on flipchart paper what the task was and discuss methods of persuasion.

11. Conclude that there are many different forms of persuasion and that it is not always easy to tell if someone is trying to persuade or influence you, especially if you like or respect them. Wanting to fit in, trying to impress and seeking validation are all reasons why a young person might do something in a gang they wouldn't do on their own.

12. Finish by reaffirming that if anyone feels that they are being persuaded or influenced by someone to do something that makes them feel uncomfortable, they should speak to an adult or someone they trust.

Snap decision

No decision

Responsible decision

INFLUENCE AND PERSUASION CASE STUDY

Part 1

Abe is 15 and lives with his mum and two sisters. He has been bought up to be respectful to women and his mum is proud that in her family domestic chores are equally shared, regardless of gender. She identifies as a feminist and expects her children to live by the same principles.

Whilst out in the community with his friends, there is an incident and the police arrive. All of the boys are taken to the police station and their parents called. Abe is embarrassed and feels misunderstood. What started off as banter between the boys and a group of girls escalated into a loud argument after one of the boys tried to kiss a girl. Abe is angry; he can't understand why he has been taken to the police station. He was just there and got caught up in it all.

When the police show him CCTV images he can't believe what he is seeing. He feels growing anxiety about what his mum will say as he watches himself on film joining in with the other lads shouting sexist comments and circling the girls, who he can now see were not enjoying the attention. How could he have said those things? It is not how he remembers it at all. He thought they were all having a laugh together, but caught on camera it looks like gang bullying. Why didn't he say something or walk away?

Part 2

Abe's mum arrives at the police station and is told what has happened. She is mortified and immediately asks if the girl is all right. Once she knows that, she turns her attention to Abe. She tells him she is ashamed of him: 'This wouldn't have happened if you didn't hang around with those boys', she says, 'I knew they were trouble the first time I met them. Now I hear that a young girl was sexually assaulted...'

'Sexually assaulted?' Abe interrupts, shocked at his mum, 'It was messing about that got out of hand, no one was sexually assaulted!'

His mum shakes her head, 'The minute that boy kissed her without consent it became sexual assault. Those boys have no respect, why would you want to be part of that?'

Abe doesn't know what to say. He wants to defend his friends, but now that the moment has passed, he thinks that his mum might be right. If he is honest he knows he does tend to behave differently when he is with them.

'I blame that music you listen to', she continues angrily, 'all those gangster videos with naked women and sexist lyrics are a bad influence on you. I can't believe you did nothing whilst your friend sexually bullied a young girl! You weren't brought up to behave like this!'

Abe hangs his head. He doesn't know what to do or say to make things better.

ACTIVITY 25: POSITIVE AND NEGATIVE PEER PRESSURE

Aim

- This discussion-based activity enables young people to explore the positive and negative power of collective and peer pressure.

Time: 30 minutes

Key vocabulary

- Positive and negative peer pressure

You will need

- Flipchart paper and marker pens

How to do it

1. Invite the young people to reflect on the groups they belong to, including friendship groups and families, and pull out the positive feelings and benefits they get from membership. This could include love, security and a sense of 'belonging'.

2. Now move on to ask:
   - Do you behave the same way in a group as you do on your own?
   - Do you behave differently with different groups?

3. Consider the differences in behaviour, for example, between being out with friends and at home with parents. Conclude that most people are multi-faceted and show different sides of themselves in different circumstances. Explain that psychologists' research suggests people are actually heavily influenced by what they see others doing.

4. Discuss in pairs a time when the young people:
   - were swayed to do something positive as part of a group
   - felt pressured to do something they didn't want to do.

   Encourage the young people to explore the reasons behind their actions and what they hoped to gain or feared to lose by going along with the crowd.

5. Invite feedback and record ideas under the headings 'Gain' and 'Lose' on flipchart paper. So, for example, a 'gain' might be peer acceptance or status, but by following the crowd you may 'lose' self-respect or the opportunity to stand up for something you believe in.

   Explain that specific things that persuade someone to do something or not do it are often referred to as risk and protective factors. Suggest that these contribute to 'peer pressure' in both positive and negative ways, which can be described as social pressure by peers to take a certain action, adopt certain values, or otherwise conform in order to be accepted. In this way being with friends involved in criminal activity can influence your own choices just as being with friends who stay out of trouble can.

   Ask: How might peer pressure influence gang behaviour? *Consider attitudes, values, beliefs and actions.*

   Suggest that whilst membership of a gang can create feelings of safety, protection and value, peer pressure within a gang can sway people to engage in less positive behaviour or even get swept along into actions they later regret.

Ask: What are the negatives of being in a gang? Examples could include:

- being accountable to them

- having to do as you're told

- fights with other gangs

- being expected to take part in initiation ceremonies

- proving loyalty could get me hurt me/'turf wars'

- bullying

- drug taking

- county lines

- law breaking activities

- losing my own sense of identity

- losing personal freedom.

6. Conclude that having confidence in yourself as an individual with your own abilities, values and beliefs is important, and that this can be difficult to maintain within any group and in particular in a gang, which is likely to have its own identity. Accept that it can be hard when there is strong peer pressure to think or behave in a certain way, but it is possible if you set and maintain your own boundaries based on your personal attitudes and values.

ACTIVITY 26: DIFFERENT FORMS OF PEER PRESSURE

Aim

- To explore different types of negative peer pressure and ways to challenge it to help build resilience.

Time: 90 minutes

Key vocabulary

- Verbal and non-verbal peer pressure
- Resilience

You will need

- Copies of the Peer Pressure Scenarios
- Paper and pens
- Mobile phones to film role-plays, social media apps to broadcast or share key messages (optional)

How to do it

1. Start by suggesting that peer pressure isn't always a negative thing as it can encourage individual and/or collective positive action, for example, to challenge inequalities or contribute to community action. On an individual level, positive peer pressure can push comfort zones and give someone an opportunity to discover something new.

   Explain that there are different forms of peer pressure that can negatively influence behaviour including spoken pressure, for example, put downs, shaming, threats and verbal coercion to put pressure on someone to do or not do something. Alternatively it can be unspoken, when nothing is said but because others are doing it there is pressure to conform and do the same, for example, socially excluding, isolating or turning negative attention on someone to exert pressure and/or control. This can happen both on and offline.

2. Divide the young people into small groups and hand group each a different scenario. Their task is to devise a short 3-minute role-play based around the scenario to explore the different types of peer pressure experienced by the characters.

   If you plan to share the learning from this via video or social media apps, set this up now. This can either be a live broadcast of the dramatic scenes and/or following discussions or record to edit later and share highlights.

3. Allow 30 minutes for preparations and then invite each group to perform their scene.

4. After each performance call 'Freeze' and invite the role-players to relax. Then facilitate a short discussion that asks the audience:

   - What forms of peer pressure did you see?
   - Why might someone give in to this peer pressure?

   Interview the actors in character:

   - How did it feel to put pressure on another person?
   - How did it feel to experience this form of peer pressure?
   - How easy was it to resist? What made it easy/hard?

Encourage the young people to identify the feelings and emotions evoked by spoken and unspoken peer pressure.

5. Conclude by saying that negative peer pressure evokes a broad emotional response including confusion, insecurity, fear, loneliness and guilt. This can have a negative impact on mental health and emotional wellbeing, especially if the pressure is to do something you are unsure of or know to be wrong.

6. Back in a circle, close the activity by asking each person to suggest one way to resist negative peer pressure in a positive, assertive way. Ideas could include:

    -   Live according to your own values by thinking ahead and considering strategies before difficulties arise.

    -   Look at the person and make eye contact before speaking.

    -   Say 'no' and mean it.

    -   Say 'no' and give a short explanation that clearly states your position.

    -   Use delay tactics to give you time.

    -   Walk away.

    -   Use positive self-talk, for example, remind yourself of why you are making a choice, why it will give the best outcome for you and coach yourself to stay strong before speaking.

    -   Use non-verbal communication to reinforce what you say, for example, firmly saying 'stop' and putting a hand up in front of you.

    -   Use a calm voice and don't be drawn into an argument.

    -   Clearly say that you don't want to engage in that activity.

    -   Suggest an alternative activity and give a reason why this is a better choice.

    -   Be clear about your personal boundaries and reinforce them regularly.

Suggest that understanding how peer pressure works and planning some potential ways to manage it can increase confidence and enable you to cope better. However, if you feel threatened or scared, get to safety and tell someone.

PEER PRESSURE SCENARIOS

Scenario One
Jade is sitting in the car with Jackson, her boyfriend. Jackson is 25 and Jade is 14 but she doesn't care about the age gap, she loves him.

Jackson has asked Jade to stay in the car and keep a look out for the police whilst he does a business deal. Jade doesn't want to. She knows that Jackson is involved in criminal activity and she doesn't want to get into trouble.

Scenario Two
Jasmine has been invited to Ayesha's birthday party. Jasmine doesn't know her that well, as Ayesha tends to hang out with a local gang, but tonight everyone is going and she doesn't want to miss out.

Soon after Jasmine arrives an older male offers her an alcoholic drink. She doesn't want a drink but fears being ridiculed by him and other gang members who are watching the exchange.

Scenario Three
Eden and Marcus grew up together and are more like brothers than friends. Both have been running errands for a local gang, and both like the protection and sense of belonging membership gives them.

Eden has been storing weapons at his house and is trying to persuade Marcus to do the same. He reminds Marcus of their friendship and questions his loyalty when he refuses.

Scenario Four
Freddie, Tom and Delilah witness a fight where a boy is seriously injured. They all know who is responsible and Freddie is ready to go to the police and make a witness statement.

Tom and Delilah tell him he is mad to even think about informing; they remind him that they all live close to where the attack happened, and warn him that those responsible are likely to take revenge.

Scenario Five
Rhiannon is with a group that regularly gathers outside the block of flats they live in. A passer-by tells them to stop making a noise and threatens to call the police. One young man shouts abuse and within seconds others join in.

Someone notices Rhiannon has kept quiet and soon the attention is turned on her, with people yelling 'chicken'.

ACTIVITY 27: POSITIVE ROLE MODELS

Aims

- To provide an example of a young man who was involved in gangs and crime but went on to become an inspiration to others.

- To explore the concept of positive role models and the impact they can have on others.

Time: 30 minutes

Key vocabulary

- Positive role model

- Choice

- Self-esteem

You will need

- Access to *The Guardian* article on Anthony Joshua[1] (please note that other positive role models can also be used)

How to do it

1. Start by asking the young people to suggest people they think provide a positive role model for the ethnicity, faith or community they represent. *For example, could include celebrities, music artists, sports people, politicians or figures known to the public for an achievement.*

    Encourage them to explain why they think their suggestions are someone who should be looked up to and admired by a younger generation.

2. Write the headline below on a large sheet of paper and display it where all of the young people will be able to see it:

    Anthony Joshua was the bad boy from a Watford council estate. Now he takes on Wladimir Klitschko with golden fists[2]

    Explain that many young people feel trapped in gang life and gang-related crime but this person proves that it is possible to make different choices and to turn your life around. Read out the headline and ask who knows anything about Anthony Joshua.

3. In pairs, set the young people the task of researching Anthony Joshua to discover how he managed to achieve so much, despite being given a prison sentence. In particular, ask them to find out:

    -   how he got into crime

    -   what influenced him to change

    -   how he changed his life.

4. Alternatively ask each pair to research and then create either a presentation using PowerPoint or to curate an Instagram or Pinterest board based around the same questions.

---

1   McRae, D. (2015) 'Anthony Joshua goes from prison to punching way to heavyweight greatness.' *The Guardian*, 26 May. Available at www.theguardian.com/sport/2015/may/26/anthony-joshua-boxing-prison-heavyweight-greatness

2   Mail Online, 29 April 2017. Available at www.dailymail.co.uk/sport/boxing/article-4457284/Joshua-dropped-bad-boy-emerge-golden-fists.html

5. Invite each group to share their findings and then facilitate a discussion that considers how Joshua's story could provide a positive role model for others.

6. Conclude that being a positive role model is about how you conduct yourself, your actions and behaviour. Invite the young people to consider the type of role model they offer younger members of their community, and why this can be important.

ACTIVITY 28: **POSITIVE FUTURES**

Aims

- To provide a positive role model who has overcome adversity.

- To identify what's important now and for the future.

- To identify a goal based on personal values.

Time: 45 minutes

Key vocabulary

- Personal values

- Positive role model

You will need

- Copies of the lyrics 'Black' by Dave[3]

- Access to music provider and speakers to play 'Black' by Dave

- Flipchart paper and marker pens or whiteboard

- A Personal Goal card and pen for each person

How to do it

1. Tell the young people that in this activity they are going to be exploring personal values – meaning what we believe in and consider important. Suggest that these provide the framework from which we devise the rules that are going to govern our lives and the choices we make.

2. Play 'Black' by Dave.

3. Read this review and then facilitate a short discussion to explore the meaning:

    > A fearless track in its entirety, in these bars Dave explicitly addresses the corruption dominating the media as it continues to paint a distorted image of black teens, also highlighting the hypocrisy in its coverage of white killers as well as the dangerously prejudiced attitudes of some police.[4]

4. Alternatively choose another track that you think will resonate more with the group, as long as the lyrics allow for a discussion about values afterwards.

5. Hand out a copy of the lyrics 'Black'.

    Ask: What do you think this song is about? What is Dave saying? *For example, inequality, racism, social inequality, stereotypes, violence etc.*

    Note down responses on a sheet of flipchart paper or a whiteboard.

    Ask: The video for the song featured prominent black Brits such as Stormzy, Raheem Sterling and fashion designer Ozwald Boateng. Why do you think they agreed to appear in it? *For example, shared values, shared experiences, pride, respect etc.*

    Ask: How might using famous people in videos like this influence the values of others? *For example, provide a positive role model, inspire and motivate etc.*

    Again, note down any ideas.

---

3   'Black' by Dave, from Psychodrama. Available at https://genius.com/Dave-black-lyrics
4   Khamis, L. (2019) 'Bar for bar: A track-by-track guide to the lyricism of Dave's Psychodrama.' Red Bull, 8 March. Available at www.redbull.com/gb-en/dave-psychodrama-lyrics

6. Encourage a general discussion on this and the impact they think this and other influential music has, positive and negative, on society and young people in particular. Suggest that through lyrics and words the artists share their values and the things that are important to inspire and motivate others.

7. Ask the young people to identify one goal for the future based on their own beliefs or values and one thing they will have to do or change to achieve it. These can be written on the Personal Goal cards and then form the basis of future work to enable the young people to reach them.

PERSONAL GOAL

Part One: My goal
This is your goal, so choose something that you would like to work on, based on your personal values and beliefs.

....

....

....

....

Part Two: My action
Identify one action you can take towards reaching your goal. Be realistic and focus on something you can do to start the process.

....

....

....

....

Part Three: My support
Identify sources of support to motivate and inspire you as you work towards your goal.

....

....

....

....

My name: .... Date: ....

ACTIVITY 29: DEVELOPING SELF-LOVE

Aims

- To explore what is meant by 'self-love'.

- To consider the differences between 'self-love' and arrogance.

- To explore how having 'self-love' builds resilience to risk-taking activities.

Time: 30 minutes

Key vocabulary

- Role models

- Self-love

- Positive choices

- Self-confidence

You will need

- Copies of the Motivational Statements

- Paper and pens

- Access to social media (optional)

How to do it

1. Begin the activity by explaining the importance of having a positive identity and feeling confident about who you are and what you stand for.

2. Divide the main group into four, giving each smaller group one of the Motivational Statements. Some of the group may have seen one or more of these before, as they are widely posted on social media. This doesn't matter.

3. Their task is to read and discuss what they think the message is behind the statement and what it is trying to say about self-love.

4. Once they have done this they should create a new Motivational Statement to motivate and inspire other young people to be more accepting and kinder to themselves in terms of their beliefs, attitudes and values.

5. Invite each group to feedback first the statement they analysed and their understanding of its meaning and then the newly devised group statement. These can then be transferred to social media to inspire others (optional).

   Explain that being arrogant and loving yourself are completely different things. Whilst some people hear 'self-love' and associate it with arrogance, egotism and/or vanity, it actually means loving and valuing the things that make us different and having self-respect, a positive self-image and self-confidence.

   Suggest that if you have self-love you are more likely to take care of yourself and those around you, making it more likely that in challenging situations you will find the strength to make the right choices and withstand things like negative peer pressure.

MOTIVATIONAL STATEMENTS

Eat like you love yourself. Move like you love yourself. Speak like you love yourself. Act like you love yourself.

Loving yourself starts with liking yourself, which starts with respecting yourself, which starts with thinking of yourself in positive ways.

Your relationship with yourself sets the tone for every other relationship you have.

Love yourself first, because that's who you'll be spending the rest of your life with.

ACTIVITY 30: CROSSING THE LINE

Aims

- To explore the impact of stress on physical and emotional wellbeing.
- To recognize emotional and physical 'cues' when a line is being crossed.
- To identify a personal network that can offer support if things get difficult.

Time: 45 minutes

Key vocabulary

- Stress
- Crossing the line
- Resilience

You will need

- Sets of Crossing the Line Triggers
- Large sheets of paper and red marker pens
- Sticky notes and pens
- Information about local support services for young people

How to do it

1. Introduce this exercise by explaining that you will be looking at stressful situations where a decision needs to be made, the physical and emotional signals the body sends to alert to stress, and positive ways to handle it.

   Ask: What is stress?

   Invite answers to be called out and explain that stress is normal and that everyone experiences it. Point out that although it's often defined as worry, tension or anxiety, not all stress is bad. Some stress, for example before a big event like a wedding, can be happy and exciting as well as challenging. Explain that too much pressure, especially if stress is triggered by fear, can be overwhelming and trigger the body into 'fight or flight' mode. Suggest that it can be hard to make the right decision when experiencing extreme stress, and that without building resilience and learning coping strategies negative stress can have a serious impact on mental health and emotional wellbeing.

2. Divide the young people into small groups. Give each person six sticky notes and a pen. Explain that when you shout 'Go!' they have 2 minutes to write down situations they think are stressful for young people, one on each sticky note. These can be anything, but suggest that if anyone wants to use a personal situation it should already have been resolved as there will not be time to offer individual support. If required, signpost to local support services.

3. Now give each group a sheet of flipchart paper and a red marker pen. Ask a volunteer from each group to turn the page portrait and then draw a thick red line across the middle of the paper. Explain that below the red line represents acceptable, normal levels of stress that everyone is likely to experience through the ups and downs of life. Above the line represents experiences likely to provoke extreme levels of stress and trigger feelings of anger, anxiety, nervousness, depression or even violence.

4. The next task is to collate all of the sticky notes and to go through each of the suggestions, discussing why it could be stressful, and then plotting it on the flipchart paper to show if they think it would provoke a stress response below or above the red line, and if so, by how much.

   Invite feedback to compare and contrast the degrees of stress identified and the circumstances around it.

5. Give out sets of Crossing the Line Triggers. The group task is to read each trigger and discuss any feelings and emotions that the situation might provoke, before plotting it above or below the red line.

6. Explain that any time our personal 'red line' is near to being crossed the body produces automatic physical and emotional cues to alert us to potential risk or danger. Being able to identify these enables us to make decisions to move away from harm and stay safe.

7. Feedback key points from each group, reinforcing the importance of recognizing automatic danger cues and taking positive action. This should always include the option to walk away.

8. Point out that it is not always easy to do the right thing but that by being self-aware and alert to automatic cues the likelihood of making positive choices increases.

9. Introduce this framework for assertiveness in challenging situations, and write it up to aid learning:

   – Use direct language to describe your concern.

   – Use 'I' statements to describe emotions and feelings, for example, 'I feel angry', rather than 'You make me angry'.

   – Actively listen to the other person's point of view.

   – Make up your mind (if you cannot do that, ask for more time or refuse to do anything until you can).

   – Express your decision – without apologizing, making excuses or justifying it, for example, 'I don't want to do that' rather than 'I'm sorry, but I don't want to do that'.

   – Once you have set a personal boundary, stick to it.

10. Summarize that everyone experiences stress as they go through life, but people find different things stressful. By better understanding the situations that stress you the most you can begin to build the resilience to be more assertive and develop strategies to cope.

CROSSING THE LINE TRIGGERS

Your friend has an argument with someone, which nearly leads to a fight. They expect you to go with them to seek revenge, regardless of the consequences.

Your friends are chanting racist abuse at a group of young people. You don't agree with the message but are being pressured to join in.

Your friend never has any money. You keep lending cash, which they have not paid back. Now they want to borrow more.

Pressure is being put on you to steal alcohol from home. You don't think this is such a good idea but don't want to lose face amongst your peers.

Your friend has 'borrowed' their mum's car. They only have a provisional license but ask you to get in the car and go for a drive.

Your best friend is skipping school to meet up with older peers. They want you to go too but you don't want to do anything that will affect your grades.

ACTIVITY 31: MANAGING STRESS

Aims

- To consider stress and the impact it can have on mental health.
- To learn positive coping skills for managing stress and anxiety to achieve healthier outcomes.

Time: 60 minutes

Key vocabulary

- Stress, stress management
- Mediation
- Relaxation

You will need

- Copies of the Relaxation Techniques
- Flipchart paper and marker pens

Facilitator note: To prepare for the session, research and download an example meditation/stress management/sleep and relaxation podcast. Please listen in advance to ensure the podcast is appropriate for the young people you are working with.

How to do it

1. Working in pairs, invite the young people to sit facing each other, ready to listen and concentrate.

2. Ask everyone to think of a recent example of a situation where someone was putting pressure on them to do something they didn't want to do. Examples could include at home, such as being told to tidy their room, get homework in on time or come in at a certain time, or out in the community, such as peer pressure to break rules.

3. Tell them to take it in turns to describe the situation they've identified and spend 3 minutes each talking about what made it stressful, the sources of stress, how they handled it and what happened. Help keep the task on track by giving a 30-second warning and then calling time at the end of 3 minutes before directing the second partner to start talking.

4. At the end of recounting their story, each person should give a personal score of between 1 and 5 on how well they managed things, with 1 being 'very badly' and 5 being 'could not have done any better'.

    At this stage there is no need to share or compare scores. Explain that the scores will be revisited towards the end of the session to review after exploring different stress management techniques.

5. Instruct each pair to join up with another couple to make a new group of four. Explain that in these groups they are going to look at different ways of coping with stress.

    Read out the following scenario:

> Jude asks his girlfriend Magda to keep cannabis at her house because he fears being arrested. At first she says 'yes' but changes her mind when she sees the large package he is asking her to hide. Jude is angry, 'Don't be stupid, you never minded looking after things before' he says. 'Just keep your mouth shut, do as you're told and it will be fine.'

'That was different. This package is much too big', she says. 'If my mum finds it she will go mad and chuck me out. If the police find it they will think I'm dealing. Either way I could get into serious trouble.'

Jude is shocked; usually he can talk Magda round. But even though he begs, charms, bullies and threatens, she won't give in. Her mum has a zero tolerance policy when it comes to drugs and Magda doesn't want to be homeless.

So the cannabis stays at Jude's house and Magda feels sick with worry that he will be arrested. He already has a criminal record so could face a prison sentence this time.

Ask: What unhealthy but common ways of dealing with stress might Magda try? *Examples could include: arguing, drinking alcohol, smoking, taking drugs, getting angry, not eating healthily, shouting or becoming withdrawn.*

Invite suggestions about the likely consequences of these negative coping strategies that can physically and emotionally harm not only the individual but also others around them.

Point out that in the scenario Magda is stressed about the choices that Jude has made, which are impacting on her life. She is worried that he will get arrested, but has no power over his decision to be in possession of an illegal substance. She is being asked to do something illegal without all of the facts, for example, who the drugs belong to, why Jude thinks he's going to be arrested etc. Suggest that stress can make you feel as though everything is spiralling out of control and that you don't know what to do for the best. Breaking the situation down to recognize the things she is responsible for and the things she has no power to change could help her to feel less stressed. Ultimately she has made a good decision and she should find sources of support to help her stick to it.

6. Ask the young people to come up with positive ideas for coping with other stressful situations and write these ideas up onto flipchart paper. These could include:

   - telling a trusted adult or contacting a professional organization

   - exploring all of the consequences and rationalizing the most likely outcomes to get things into perspective

   - taking time out to calm down

   - listening to music

   - writing things down to literally look at from all angles

   - talking it through with a friend

   - using some basic relaxation techniques.

7. Return to the scenario:

After a week of constant arguing, Magda finds the strength to finish with Jude. It was a difficult choice and she knows that he won't easily let her go, but she reasons that it is the best decision for her. Gang life looked exciting but now she knows the realities, she is just relieved that she didn't get too involved.

Suggest that even though Magda has made the brave choice to walk away from Jude and the gang, she could still experience stress as a result of the trauma. Ask young people to identify why this may be, for example, fear of retaliation, the pain of breaking up with someone, anxiety that Jude will be caught by the police, worry that she will be drawn back in by other gang members etc. Conclude that it will be important for Magda to surround herself with positive friendships and develop the skills and strategies to cope with future stress in healthy ways. This will help to reduce any longer-term damage to her mental health, including post-traumatic stress disorder (PTSD).

Remind the young people that anyone involved with, or at risk from, gangs who needs help can call the NSPCC helpline on 0808 800 5000. Helpline practitioners can offer confidential advice, support and information.

8. Introduce the idea of relaxation and mindfulness techniques to help combat stress and aid sleep. Explain the importance of finding one that suits you. Give out the Relaxation Techniques handout for the young people to take home and try out. Suggest that a good place to start is to sit or lie quietly and if possible dim the lights to practise mindfulness. Many people find meditation a useful way to combat stress, and there are lots of free ones available free of charge to download from iTunes, BBC Sounds and other podcast providers, including:

    –   'Therapy for Black Girls', Joy Harden-Bradford, PhD

    –   'PLT: Behind closed doors', Pretty Little Things

    –   'Yoga download', 20-minute yoga sessions, YogaDownload.com

    –   'Tracks to Relax', Guided sleep meditations

    –   'The Daily Meditation Podcast', Mary Meckley

    –   'White Light Mediation', Sandeep Khurana.[5]

9. Suggest that the young people find their own favourite online podcast/soundscape or chill mix and report back on its effectiveness to their peers, either face-to-face or via social media.

10. Finally, ask the young people to return to their original pairs to revisit the stressful situations they discussed at the start. Invite them to reflect on what they have learned to see if there are other ways they could have handled the situation to achieve a better outcome. Suggest they try some of the new techniques next time to build up their resilience to stress.

---

5   The podcasts listed are for information only; inclusion does not constitute a recommendation.

RELAXATION TECHNIQUES

Below are some relaxation techniques to try to help you relax.

Visual relaxation

- First, close your eyes.
- Then, breathe deeply and slowly, in and out.
- Think of a peaceful place, somewhere you know and feel safe.
- Imagine yourself in that place.
- Try to use each of your senses in turn (sight, hearing, smell, taste and touch).
- Hold the image as long as possible.
- Let it go, then focus on your deep breathing again.
- Repeat until you feel calm and relaxed (do this as many times as you like).
- Slowly open your eyes.
- Give yourself a few moments to adjust, taking the calm feelings with you into the rest of your day.

Physical relaxation

- Find a peaceful, quiet place.
- Lie flat on your back and close your eyes.
- Place a hand on your stomach so you can feel as you breathe in slowly and deeply, and then exhale, making sure you empty all the air from your lungs.
- Repeat six times.
- Begin tensing up different muscles one at a time (right hand, left hand, right arm, left arm etc.).
- Hold each tensing of the muscle to the count of 10.
- Then slowly release the tension to the count of 10 and relax the muscle.
- Move on to do the same with your face, neck and shoulders.
- Finish with repeating the breathing exercise.

Deep breathing meditation

- Find a peaceful, quiet place.
- Then breathe deeply and slowly, in and out.
- Clear your mind of all thoughts (imagine a thought is floating away when it comes into your head).
- Hold your concentration for as long as possible. This will increase with practice.

ACTIVITY 32: COULD, WOULD, SHOULD

Aims

- To explore gang-related dilemmas and identify available choices to stay safe.
- To better understand the decision-making process.

Time: 45 minutes

Key vocabulary

- Gangs
- Choices
- Consequences

You will need

- Copies of the Could, Would, Should Scenarios
- Paper and pens

How to do it

1. Ask the young people if they can think of a time when they made a choice they later regretted or felt was the wrong decision, for example, taking something that wasn't theirs and later discovering the impact the loss had on someone they care about, or witnessing bullying and not calling it out. Conclude that it is not always easy to do the right thing and sometimes, in challenging situations, we know what we should do but for lots of reasons we do something different.

2. Divide the main group into smaller groups of twos or threes. Hand each group a Could, Would, Should Scenario and paper to make notes on. Their task it to read the scenario and then discuss:

   - all of the things they could do in the same situation

   - the likely consequences of each action (positive or negative)

   - the course of action they think the character would be most likely to take.

   Allow up to 20 minutes' discussion time and then bring everyone together.

3. Invite each group to first read their scenario and the dilemmas it provokes, the choices they have identified, potential consequences and finally the action they would take. Afterwards invite individual comments from the wider group, especially if someone would have made a different choice.

4. Now suggest that there is an option for each dilemma you find yourself in, which is what you 'should do'. Go back to the scenarios to see if the choices made all reflect the legally, morally or socially 'right thing' to do. If not, explore the internal and external factors that might impact on choices made. For example, in the scenario where a young person is being paid to courier drugs, the right thing to do in a health emergency is to tell the paramedics exactly what has been taken to preserve life. However, selfish fears about losing money or concerns about personal safety from gang punishment or worry about potentially being arrested may lead someone to doing the 'wrong thing' by keeping quiet.

Facilitate a discussion that considers:

- What are the possible consequences of making the 'wrong' or 'right' choice? *For example, the impact on physical and mental health; the effect decisions can have on everyone involved; the short- and longer-term implications etc.*

- What affects the decision-making process? *For example, the opinions of friends and family; personal values; community culture; previous experiences etc.*

- What support is there for making the right choice? Encourage the young people to consider their personal support networks as well as online support, *for example, from Childline, or other professional organizations.*

5. Conclude that doing the right thing is not always easy, but there can be negative consequences for taking what might appear to be the easy way out. Stress the importance of always considering the potential consequences before making a decision, and remind them that there is always a choice.

Suggest that thinking things through and asking for help and support before making a difficult decision makes it more likely they will have an outcome they can live with.

COULD, WOULD, SHOULD SCENARIOS

Scenario One

Jamie is making good money carrying packages from one side of his estate to the other for a local gang. He tells himself that as long as he doesn't know exactly what is in the packages, he isn't doing anything wrong.

Tonight a young girl collapses after using drugs that he couriered in the community. He is there when the ambulance arrives and the paramedic asks if anyone knows what she has taken. Jamie has more packages in his bag so could easily tell them, but he hesitates.

What could Jamie do?

. . . .

. . . .

What will he do?

. . . .

. . . .

Scenario Two

TJ is babysitting her little brother when she gets a message from her boyfriend, Nate, asking if he can come round. He tells her the police are after him and he needs somewhere to lie low for a bit. TJ refuses, her baby brother is still awake and she doesn't want him involved. She can imagine how scared he would be if the police raid the house, and tells Nate it's a risk she isn't willing to take.

Nate feels frustrated and angry. He tells TJ it will be her fault if he gets arrested. He says that if she loves him, she will help him hide from the law.

What could TJ do?

. . . .

. . . .

What will she do?

. . . .

. . . .

Scenario Three

Joe looks up to his older brother, Jay, who is an elder in a local gang. In their area gang life is respected and it's important to belong, so he is pleased when his brother introduces him as a new recruit. With his brother to guide him he can start to make something of himself.

Last night a young man was stabbed and Joe's mum is sick with worry. She tells him that she fears for her boys every time they go out and begs Joe to reassure her that he and Jay are not involved in a gang.

What could Joe do?

. . . .

. . . .

What will he do?

. . . .

. . . .

Scenario Four

Zack and Danny used to be best friends at primary school but since they went to different secondary schools they've drifted apart. Zack is now part of the local gang whilst Danny is studying hard to get into university, as he wants to be a doctor.

Today Zack finds Danny caught up in an argument with other gang members. The noise is escalating and it looks like there will be a fight. He can see Danny is outnumbered and knows that the other boys carry knives.

What could Zack do?

. . . .

. . . .

What will he do?

. . . .

. . . .

Scenario Five

Molly's boyfriend Tariq belongs to a local gang. She doesn't agree with everything the gang does but Tariq swears he isn't involved. He says he only hangs out with them for protection and is so kind and loving when they are together, she believes him.

Sammy, Molly's best friend, tells her Tariq physically threatened a young man over an unpaid drug debt. She says that Tariq is well known for violence and when Molly accuses Sammy of lying, she issues an ultimatum; split up with Tariq or their friendship is over.

What could Molly do?

. . . .

. . . .

What will she do?

. . . .

. . . .

ACTIVITY 33: PRESSURE POINTS

Aims

- To identify potential triggers that could escalate into an aggressive and/or violent situation.
- To discuss positive strategies for reducing conflict to stay safe.

Time: 60 minutes

Key vocabulary

- Triggers
- Anger
- Aggressive behaviour
- Violence

You will need

- A selection of photographs that show young people in a range of situations
- Whiteboard or flipchart paper and marker pens
- A2 sheets of paper and pens
- A5 sheets of paper
- Pairs of scissors
- Social media sharing platforms (optional)

Facilitator note: Before the session, go online to find photos that show a range of diverse situations where arguments, tensions or aggressive behaviour could escalate into gang-related violence.

How to do it

1. Prepare for the session by displaying the photographs at different points in the room. When the young people arrive, explain that the focus for this activity is to identify triggers for anger, aggression and violence.

2. Invite them to look at all the photographs and then to stand by the one that resonates most. Once you have groups of no more than six, tell them to remove the picture from the wall and sit down. Ask the newly formed groups to look carefully at their chosen photograph and discuss why it appealed so much and what emotions they think are displayed by the figures in it.

3. Invite feedback and write up the feelings and emotions identified as a word cloud on flipchart paper or a whiteboard. These could include:

   - frustration
   - confusion
   - fear
   - rage
   - sorrow
   - anger
   - pressure.

4. Conclude that each photograph shows a clip from a story that ends in a violent confrontation that will later be reported in the media as a gang-related crime.

5. Give out A2 sheets of paper and pens. Instruct a volunteer from each group to take their paper and fold it in half and then half again, repeating until they have created eight A6 squares when opened up.

6. Explain that now they know the ending of the story, their next task is to devise an eight-frame portrait storyboard in a graphic novel style that explains the steps it took to get from what is happening in their photograph to the violent conclusion. Allow up to 45 minutes for the graphic novel to develop and encourage the young people to be creative and really think through the scene. Who is the aggressor? Who is the victim? What is the conflict over? Is any peer pressure involved? It is up to them if other characters join in, whether weapons are used and how serious any injury sustained is, but what is required is that they explain exactly what happened to trigger each stage along the way. This can be shown using speech or thought bubbles etc. as well as pictures. Suggest they use the feelings and emotions already identified as a reference.

7. Call time and ask each group to stick their original photograph on the wall and then display their storyboard next to it. In turn invite each group to present the entire sequence of events they have created, starting with their interpretation of what's happening in the photograph to the conclusion of their story in the final frame.

8. Facilitate a review of what has been shown and the triggers identified that escalated the situation. These could include:

   - feeling humiliated, belittled or embarrassed

   - feeling trapped

   - demonstrating physical power over someone weaker

   - lashing out to get away

   - lashing out in anger

   - using violence as a threat to make somebody do something they don't want to.

   In particular, if weapons were used, focus on the moments leading up to this to consider if it was a deliberate choice or happened in the heat of the moment.

9. Then ask each group to reflect on their story to identify if there was a point when those involved in the conflict had a choice to back down or choose not to use a weapon. Again, ask each group to share their thoughts. Triggers may include:

   - name calling

   - miscommunication

   - insults to friends or family

   - incitement to violence from others

   - challenging strength or ability

   - invasion of personal space

   - physical touch, for example, a push, slap or shove.

10. Explain that being able to recognize triggers, and understand your own, makes it more likely that you handle confrontation without it escalating to violent outbursts.

    With this information, hand out some scissors and an A5 sheet of paper to each group. Instruct them to cut out the last two frames at the bottom of their A2 storyboard, putting them to one side. They should now turn the A5 sheet of paper landscape and fold it in half. Opened out, this can now be used to add to the story.

Their task is to reimagine the escalation phase of the conflict, this time identifying the triggers and resolving it in a way that avoids violence. This can be drawn and annotated (as before) on the two new frames created with the A5 paper.

11. Again, share the new endings, explaining the choices made and how these contribute to a more positive conclusion. Make sure these include the option to walk away and/or call the police. Encourage suggestions as to why people might not do this, for example not wanting to lose face, notions of loyalty or the belief that you should stand and fight, making it clear that this is not a valid reason to put yourself and/or others at risk, especially as you may not know if the other person is armed.

Encourage the young people to trust their instincts. Stress that leaving a potentially volatile situation before it can escalate is the safest course of action, and that being able to recognize triggers helps in making the best decisions for yourself and for others.

12. Reassemble the storyboards to show the original photograph at the top, above the first six frames of the storyboard, followed by a gap and then the two alternative endings.

13. Consider sharing these on social media platforms, along with messages that reflect learning about triggers and choice etc., to raise awareness with peers and contribute to other anti-knife crime messages.

ACTIVITY 34: ANGER AND VIOLENCE EXPLORED

Aims

- To identify causes of violence and the links between anger and violence.
- To consider strategies to manage anger non-violently.

Time: 60 minutes

Key vocabulary

- Anger
- Escalation
- Violence

You will need

- Flipchart paper and marker pens
- Sticky tack

How to do it

1. Split the young people into three groups and give each group some flipchart paper and marker pens. Explain that they have 15 minutes to consider three topics, after which each group will be invited to present their ideas on one, considering the following questions:

   - Where do we see violence?
   - What does violence look like?
   - When is violence most likely to occur?

2. Call time and facilitate feedback, allowing other groups to comment and add to each presentation.

   Acknowledge that anger is a valid emotion and that everyone feels angry some times. Emphasize that it is not the emotion that sometimes causes problems, but how we react to it and behave.

   Suggest that anger is a common cause of violence, but make it clear that not all anger leads to violence. Facilitate a wordstorm to identify some of the factors that can lead up to a violent outburst, for example:

   - a desire to feel powerful
   - losing control of emotions
   - feeling trapped or cornered
   - alcohol or drug misuse
   - not wanting to back down
   - having a 'hard' reputation to maintain.

   Record ideas on a sheet of flipchart paper and display it so the young people can see it.

3. Now ask everyone to close their eyes and to think back to the last time they felt really angry, for example, an argument with parents, a friend or a situation where they felt disrespected. Encourage the young people to concentrate hard on the memory, visualizing what led up to the incident, thinking about what triggered the argument, how it felt in the moment as they became angry and then what they did during the angry phase.

4. Whilst this is happening take four fresh sheets of flipchart paper. Write the headings: 'Think' on paper one, 'Feel' on paper two, 'Physical' on paper three and 'Do' on paper four, and then put them to one side.

5. Invite the young people to open their eyes and to give you a brief synopsis of the triggers that sparked the angry situation. Write these up under the heading 'Triggers' on another sheet of flipchart paper. At this stage do not make any comments.

6. Next, in turn, ask the young people to describe the thoughts they had as an automatic response to the situation that triggered their anger. Record suggestions on the sheet of paper headed 'Think'. For example, **Trigger:** Overhearing someone insult you. **Think:** 'How dare they?' 'They are asking for trouble', 'They are not showing me enough respect', 'They deserve to be punished'.

7. Move on to ask the young people to share the emotional response they had to the trigger situation. Explain that a negative emotional reaction follows negative automatic thoughts. Record these contributions on paper under the heading 'Feelings'. For example, **Feel:** frustration, anger, rage, out of control, like you're going to explode.

8. Next, ask the young people to tell you the physical response and biological changes they experienced during the episode, and write them up on sheet three under the heading 'Physical'. For example, **Physical:** breathing hard, going red in the face, rapid heartbeat or becoming tearful.

9. Finally, ask what they actually did to cope with the feelings of anger and write these up on the last sheet of paper under the heading 'Do'. Explain that negative automatic thoughts, emotions and physical symptoms can result in things like shouting, arguing, criticizing, verbally, throwing/breaking objects, or in extreme cases, physically attacking another person. There are other responses, including turning anger inwards and self-harming, but this exercise focuses on understanding the 'think, feel, physical, do' model to find more positive ways to resolve conflict situations to avoid violence.

10. Take all five of the sheets of paper and stick them on a wall in this order:

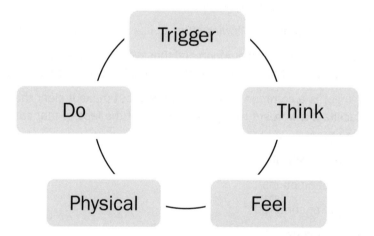

Explain that this model shows how a trigger can escalate quickly from negative thoughts to negative feelings to physiological changes that spark aggressive or even violent action. The thing to learn is how to put a block in at different points in the cycle to allow space to think and make better decisions.

11. Give out more paper and ask each group to draw the model in the centre of the paper, leaving plenty of space around the circle. Next, instruct them to select one of the angry situations previously discussed to test against the model, using a coloured pen to explore their responses to the trigger and what happened.

12. Ask them to repeat, but this time, imagine a big red stop sign flashed up at the 'Think' stage. They should then use the following four questions to test the validity of the negative thoughts that fuelled feelings, physical changes and ultimately their behaviour:

   – Question 1: What am I thinking?

   – Question 2: Is it true?

   – Question 3: Where is my evidence?

   – Question 4: What do I want from this situation?

13. Using a different coloured pen, ask each group to use the answers from the four questions to inform the rest of the process. Ask:

   – How did testing the evidence impact on feelings? *For example, being able to put things into perspective; recognizing the part of other people in escalating a situation; realizing that the anger is fuelled by past experiences; reflecting that the information you have is incomplete and you don't know the full story; understanding that your anger is unjust etc.*

   – How did thinking things through impact on physical responses? *For example, getting things into perspective slowed down the escalation phase etc.*

   – How did knowing what you wanted from the situation impact on behaviour? *For example, being able to express emotions; saying what you want/feel; putting your side of the argument without shouting; being able to walk away etc.*

Explain that by stopping to think through the questions it's possible to create enough space between thinking and feeling to consider the potential consequences of different responses before choosing what to do, which could lead to a more positive outcome. It is also likely to slow down the physical reaction to anger triggers, reducing the anger cues the brain receives from increased blood pressure and the 'fight or flight' signals, making a violent response less likely.

The next step is to choose how to respond assertively rather than aggressively, giving back ownership and control in the situation. The more this technique is used, the more natural it becomes to take a breath and think before acting, so encourage the young people to start trying it out the next time they are in a conflict situation.

ACTIVITY 35: MANAGING ANGER

Aims

- To better understand the fight, flight or freeze reaction.
- To understand how anger triggers affect responses in angry, aggressive or violent situations.
- To identify personal anger triggers.

Time: 60 minutes

Key vocabulary

- Fight
- Flight
- Freeze
- Anger
- Personal anger triggers

You will need

- Whiteboard or flipchart paper and marker pens
- Copies of the Anger Triggers worksheet and pens

How to do it

1. Explain that the brain has a full-time alarm system that is constantly looking out for potential threats. This can help to keep us safe by alerting us to danger by triggering a 'flight, flight or freeze' response, which is a series of physical changes within the body designed to give a burst of energy and strength to either 'fight' or get away. The sympathetic nervous system and hormones such as cortisol, adrenaline and noradrenalin released into the blood stream regulate these responses. Once the acute stress is over the body returns to its normal relaxed state. The time this takes depends on the person, so it is important to give someone space after an argument whilst they literally 'cool off'.

2. Divide a sheet of flipchart paper (or use a whiteboard) into three, and write the headings 'Flight', 'Fight' and 'Freeze'. Invite suggestions of examples to go under each heading and record for later. For example:

   - Flight: Running away, emotionally distancing, ignoring the situation, being indecisive etc.

   - Fight: Shouting, yelling, arguing, swearing, throwing things, hitting etc.

   - Freeze: Stopping, refusing to be drawn into an argument, emotionally withdrawing, distraction techniques etc.

   Suggest that whilst we all have the same fight, flight or freeze response, the triggers we respond to and the degree to which we respond differ based on things like our general personality, learned responses, culture, faith and values and previous experiences. People who have experienced past traumatic life events, particularly in childhood, can be in a state of hyper-arousal and easily triggered into a fight or flight response. This goes some way to explaining anger that seems to come out of nowhere, unexpected violent outbursts etc. Examples of past traumatic life events include witnessing domestic abuse, children witnessing the violence and horror of war or gang violence, emotional, sexual or physical abuse and neglect.

3. Give each person a copy of the Anger Triggers worksheet and a pen. These should be completed individually by putting a tick next to any of the triggers likely to 'push your buttons', that is, provoke an angry response. Point out that there are no prizes for ticking all or none of the boxes as each person will have an individual response so the number of buttons pushed will vary.

4. Divide into small groups and ask the young people to share their worksheets to identify:

    –   the top three things that 'push their buttons'

    –   how it feels when these buttons are pushed

    –   how they are likely to behave in response.

5. Allow 15 minutes for discussion and then invite each group to feedback their findings. Consider the following:

    –   We all respond to different triggers.

    –   Pushing 'anger buttons' can release positive and negative memories of previous situations.

    –   No one 'makes' you angry.

    –   When a person's anger 'buttons' are pushed, they have a choice in how they respond and they are responsible for any actions taken.

6. Instruct the young people to go back into their groups to start developing strategies for managing the situations triggered by anger buttons being pushed. Suggest that practising anticipating, exploring and expressing the emotions and actions likely to be evoked in conflict situations can help build confidence to cope positively if they happen in real life.

7. Allow 10–15 minutes for discussion and then as a whole group, pull together a charter for positively managing situations that provoke angry feelings based on the strategies they identify. Make it clear that the type of response should reflect levels of danger and potential for escalation into violence, and that getting away from the situation to stay safe should always take priority.

    Strategies for managing conflict situations could include:

    –   walking away

    –   counting to 10 before responding

    –   taking a deep breath

    –   positive self-talk (i.e., reminding yourself of a time when you managed conflict well, coaching yourself to stay calm etc.)

    –   assertively stating the problem, saying how you feel (owning it, not saying 'you make me angry when you…') and suggesting a solution

    –   finding a compromise.

ANGER TRIGGERS

Have a look at the situations below. If it is likely to push your 'anger button' place a tick next to it.

Being told lies	
Being disbelieved when you're telling the truth	
Constantly failing at something	
Someone borrowing your things without asking	
Someone insulting your family	
Someone spreading rumours about you	
Your favourite team losing an important match	
Seeing your ex with someone else	
Discovering you've been cheated on	
Not getting a job you think you deserve	
Discovering something is broken when you come to use it	
Being humiliated or belittled	
Forgetting to do something important	
People breaking their promises	
Not being able to find something you need	
Being with angry friends	
Being ignored when you try to speak	
Being rejected by someone you fancy	
Being laughed at	
Someone staring at you	
Being physically threatened	
Having a mistake you made pointed out	
Someone refusing to do what you want them to	
Getting blamed for something you didn't do	

ACTIVITY 36: BLAME AND RESPONSIBILITY

Aims

- To consider the responsibility that parents/carers have for keeping their children away from gangs.
- To encourage personal responsibility for choices made.

Time: 45 minutes

Key vocabulary

- Blame
- Parental and personal responsibility
- Consequences

You will need

- A4 paper and pens
- Parental Responsibility Scenarios
- Internet access to show the article from The Liverpool Echo[6]

How to do it

1. Show the film linked to The Liverpool Echo article. The page headline is: 'The video every parent must watch on how drugs gangs target children.'

    Afterwards ask:

    -   Do you agree that 'every parent' should watch this? Why, or why not?

    -   What responsibility do you think parents have to prevent their children getting involved with gangs?

    -   How much influence do you think they have over the choices their child makes?

    Define 'parent' as any adult who has parental responsibility for the child, which could be one or more biological parent but could also mean a foster carer, older sibling, grandparent or other family member or a corporate parent, for example, a named social worker.

    Point out that parents have a responsibility for their child until they are 18. Examples of parental responsibilities include:

    -   providing a home

    -   protecting the child and looking after their property

    -   making any decisions about medical treatment and education

    -   financially providing for the child

    -   naming the child and agreeing to any name change

    -   disciplining the child.

2. Divide the main group into groups of four, giving each group paper, pens and one of the Parental Responsibility Scenarios. Explain that the concerns shared in the scenarios by the different parents may or may not be founded, but the situation is causing arguments and stress at home.

---

6   www.liverpoolecho.co.uk/news/liverpool-news/modern-day-slavery-warning-video-14856953

3. The task for each group is to write a response, advising the parent(s) how to resolve the situation. To do this they will need to:

    –   identify any risk factors for the young person

    –   consider what the consequences might be for both the young person and the parent if nothing is done

    –   advise the parent(s) what to do next.

4. Invite each group in turn to read both the scenario and their advice and then ask the rest of the group:

    –   How practical is this advice?

    –   How do you think the child/young person will respond?

    –   Do you think it will reduce the risks?

    –   Is there anything else that could be done to reduce tension, keep everyone safe and resolve the situation?

    Advice for parents about talking to their children about gangs could include:

    –   reminding their child that they do have a choice, even if it doesn't feel like it

    –   staying calm

    –   not making accusations or threats

    –   asking questions and showing interest in the answers

    –   listening without interrupting

    –   trying to understand the situation from their point of view and why they have joined the gang

    –   asking what they can do to help, rather than telling them what to do

    –   pointing out the risks and consequences of carrying/using weapons

    –   presenting choices of what to do next

    –   offering to help find appropriate support, including from the police

    –   supporting decisions made

    –   working with them to find alternatives to being in the gang.

5. Bring the young people back together in a seated circle. Ask: Who else might have a responsibility to stop children and young people joining gangs? *Ideas could include the police, government, schools, youth workers etc. Make sure that personal responsibility is mentioned here.*

6. Refer back to the scenarios and for each consider: What responsibility do the young people involved have for the choices they make?

7. Conclude that whilst there are other factors that contribute to the situation they are in, including parents/carers, the person who is ultimately responsible for the choices we make is ourselves. (Activity 37 explores this further to learn assertiveness skills to make positive choices in difficult situations.)

PARENTAL RESPONSIBILITY SCENARIOS

Scenario One: Nick (father) and Sunni (aged 15)

Nick is very worried about his 15-year-old son, Sunni. Always a good football player who played at county level until a few months ago, Sunni now has no interest in sports and gets angry if Nick asks him why. Instead, Sunni spends most of his time roaming about with a large group of young men that Nick doesn't like.

Nick says: 'I don't know the lads, but they have a reputation on the estate for being troublemakers. I've been told that most of them have a criminal record and I don't want Sunni wasting his life hanging about with them.'

Sunni says: 'I don't know why Dad hates them so much but he gets angry if I even mention their names. I've decided it's easier not to tell him where I'm going than telling him and having a row. It's my life and I can live it how I choose.'

Scenario Two: Laura (foster carer) and Evie (aged 16)

Laura is concerned about Evie's much older boyfriend, Will. She sees him every night, coming home very late smelling of alcohol and refusing to say where she's been. Laura has heard that Will is part of a gang and that he was arrested for an assault on another young man, but Evie swears Will didn't do it.

Laura says: 'Evie is constantly looking at her phone – it's like she can't even stand up if he hasn't told her she can. I've tried talking to her but she doesn't want to listen, she's obsessed with him.'

Evie says: 'Will treats me so well, he really cares for me – more than anyone else ever has. He looks after me and I just want to be with him. Laura is just jealous because I have someone that loves me and she doesn't. He talks to me like an adult and I'm sick of being treated like a kid.'

ACTIVITY 37: TAKING RESPONSIBILITY

Aims

- To consider the challenges in taking responsibility for your actions.
- To encourage personal responsibility for choices made.

Time: 60 minutes

Key vocabulary

- Blame
- Personal responsibility
- Assertiveness
- Consequences

You will need

- A4 paper and pens
- Copies of the Taking Responsibility Scenarios
- 2 sheets of A4 paper, headed 'Easy to take responsibility' and 'Not so easy to take responsibility'

How to do it

1. Bring the young people together in a seated circle. Place one of the headed sheets of A4 paper on one side of the floor between the seats and the other on the opposite side, to create a continuum. Explain that you will be looking at a range of gang-related scenarios that will need an assertive approach to make a positive choice. Suggest that this can be especially difficult when it involves standing up to those you are close to and consider to be friends.

2. Give everyone a Taking Responsibility Scenario, but at this stage ask that they do not read it. Once everyone has a scenario invite each person to read it aloud and then respond by explaining how someone could take responsibility for their actions and make a positive choice. They should then get up and place the scenario somewhere on the continuum between 'Easy to take responsibility' and, 'Not so easy to take responsibility' based on their assessment of the situation.

3. After each placement explore attitudes to loyalty, betrayal and blame using these prompts:
   - How easy is it to stand against the crowd? What makes it harder/easier?
   - If you are paid to do something should you do it, even if you know it's wrong?
   - Is 'carrying out orders' ever a justification for breaking the law?
   - Is it reasonable to expect complete loyalty from a friend?
   - Can there be a 'collective blame' when something goes wrong?

4. Then ask if, after listening to everybody's contribution, they are happy for the scenario to remain in its original place on the continuum or if they would like to reposition it and invite reasons why/ why not to be shared.

5. Facilitate a short discussion that moves on to look at the issue of passing the blame and taking responsibility for our own actions. Discuss the difficulties involved in standing up for what you believe is right, especially if this goes against what others are doing.

6. Suggest that communicating what you think, feel or want to do assertively in challenging situations can help. Explain that assertive behaviour is based on the belief that your wants and needs are important, but not more so than the wants and needs of others. This is very different to aggressive behaviour, where the belief that your wants and needs are more important than those of others can lead to put downs, bullying and even physical violence to get your own way. The opposite of aggressive behaviour is passive behaviour, which arises from the belief that your wants and needs are less important than those of other people. If you behave in passive ways you are less likely to say what you really think or need, making it easier for others to push you into things you are uncomfortable with or to go along with the crowd.

    To be assertive in a difficult situation you have to:

    –   know what you want

    –   know your boundaries and be prepared to stick to them

    –   communicate clearly

    –   stay calm

    –   be prepared to walk away to stay safe.

    Ask: Are some people more naturally assertive than others?

7. Move the seats away and ask the young people to form an 'assertiveness line', with those who believe themselves to be very assertive at one end through to those who think they are naturally more passive in challenging situations. Then divide them into threes by asking one from the head of the assertiveness line to join with two people standing by the passive end. This will enable both perspectives to be heard in the next part of the session.

8. Explain that this is a role-play exercise, where two people will practise assertiveness and one person will observe to give feedback on the exchange. Roles will be swapped so that everyone has opportunities to experience them. Give each group three of the Taking Responsibility Scenarios previously discussed, and ask them to use assertive behaviour to make a positive choice and stay safe.

    Allow 2 minutes for each scene and then stop and allow time for observer feedback. Reinforce the following points:

    –   You have the right to say 'no' when people ask you to do something illegal, dishonest, against your beliefs or when you simply do not want to do it.

    –   You don't have to be rude, confrontational or derogatory to be assertive.

    –   Being able to manage conflict calmly can help avoid it escalating and so stay safe.

    –   Assertively saying what you think and making decisions based on your personal values and beliefs will make it easier to take responsibility for your actions.

9. Conclude that most people do not fall clearly into one category or another and will use a variety of behaviour styles depending on the situation and the people involved. Suggest that acting assertively is a way of developing self-respect and self-worth. If you value yourself, believing you are worthy of the respect and dignity you treat others with, you are less likely to take risks that are harmful. The more you do it, the stronger you become, making it less likely that you will give in to negative peer pressure.

    Suggest that young people take opportunities to practise being assertive to make them better able to cope in challenging situations.

TAKING RESPONSIBILITY SCENARIOS

You know who is dealing drugs to younger children. You want to stop it but don't want to get in trouble with the gang he works for.

Your brother comes home with blood all over his clothes, which clearly isn't his. He asks you to say that he was at home with you all night.

Your boyfriend is putting pressure on you to keep a package at your house for safekeeping. He says the police are less likely to find it there.

You borrowed money and are being pressured to pay it back, along with high interest. When you say you can't pay, they threaten you with violence.

Your foster parent tells you about a local street robbery. You know who is responsible but have been sworn to secrecy.

Your friends are responsible for graffiti in the local park. The police stop you but the only way to prove your innocence is to tell them who really did it.

Some young women are exchanging sexual favours for drugs. You think it's wrong but if you say something you are likely to lose their trust.

You are the youngest in your peer group. A robbery is planned and because of your size they are counting on you to get in through a side window.

Your sister's ex is bribing you to deliver drugs to a gang in the next town. If you don't they will post intimate pictures of her all over social media.

You had a fight and your dad threatens to find the other person involved and get revenge. You are too scared to tell him you started it.

Someone is insulting your family. They say that if you really cared about it you would stand up for them by fighting.

Section Four

STAYING SAFE

ACTIVITY 38: UNDERSTANDING VULNERABILITY

Aims

- To understand what is meant by vulnerability.

- To explore why some children and young people are more vulnerable to gangs than others.

Time: 60 minutes

Key vocabulary

- Basic needs

- Gang

- Grooming

- Vulnerability

You will need

- Internet access

- Flipchart paper and marker pens

- Copies of the Case Study: Tom's Life

How to do it

1. Read out this quote from an interview with an ex-gang member talking about why he got involved:

   > When your basic needs are not met you are likely to go elsewhere to find them. My basic needs were not met by society or at home. I got them from these people who were not good for me.[1]

   Ask:

   – What basic needs do you think he is talking about? *For example, love, loyalty, respect, money, culture and identity.*

   – Why are they considered important? *For example, to feel good about yourself, to have something to do and someone to do it with, and belonging.*

   Write the basic needs identified up on flipchart paper to refer back to later.

2. Set up the activity by dividing the young people into groups and giving out flipchart paper and marker pens. Ask a volunteer from each group to draw the outline of a large gingerbread person in the middle of the paper.

3. Next give out copies of the case study, 'Tom's Life' and allow time for it to be read. Set each group the task of reflecting on the case study to identify any factors they think make Tom more vulnerable to grooming by a gang member. External factors can be written outside the gingerbread person and internal factors on the inside. These could include:

   – **External:** local area/housing, attitude to crime by community, hanging around with older peers, peers involved with offending, poverty, education, peer group, parental substance misuse, lack of parental boundaries/too strict boundaries, money/poverty, lack of education, training and employment etc.

---

1 Taken from Gordon, A. (2018) "'I stopped learning the violin and started selling drugs": Former gang members reveal how they got sucked into London's deadly world of crime.' Mail Online, 9 April. Available at www.dailymail.co.uk/news/article-5585419/Former-gang-members-reveal-got-sucked-Londons-deadly-world-crime.html

- **Internal:** impulsive behaviour, challenging relationships at home, self-esteem, assertiveness skills, mental health, substance misuse etc.

Allow time for discussions and then invite each group to present their findings back to the rest of the group.

Ask: What other factors can make young people vulnerable to joining a gang?

There are many reasons why young people join gangs. Research suggests that these are common risk factors:

- association with known offenders/criminals

- family breakdown/poor relationships with parents

- older siblings already gang members

- poor self-esteem and low self-image

- loneliness and isolation

- living in an area where gangs operate

- being involved in gang-related activities (e.g. drug taking)

- lack of access to positive social activities (e.g. youth services, sports and community groups)

- lack of positive role models

- lack of positive friendships

- poor attachment to school/community

- difficulties at school.

4. Go back to the basic needs previously identified, and ask the young people to consider if Tom's basic needs are currently being met and how joining a gang might fulfil some of them. Reasons for him joining a gang are likely to include:

- isolation

- lack of a positive male role model

- no sense of belonging etc.

Suggest that this is why Tom is so vulnerable. Children and young people may think that being in a gang will give them security, protection and a sense of belonging, but the reality can be very different. Being in a gang puts children and young people at more risk of:

- sexual exploitation

- committing crime

- dealing or taking drugs

- entering the criminal justice system

- a criminal record (including custodial sentences)

- being a victim and/or perpetrator of violence or even death.

5. Back in their groups, set the young people the new task of identifying things that could provide Tom with more positive ways to achieve the basic needs he is currently missing. This should be based on what is available in their local area, but could include:

- counselling

- finding a mentor

- joining a sports club

- youth clubs or projects

Make the following points:

- Some researchers think that there are specific risks and vulnerabilities that make a young person more susceptible to gangs than their peers.

- The vulnerabilities identified could make Tom more open to grooming by a gang but they do not mean he will definitely join.

- Getting involved in positive activities that increase his self-confidence and self-esteem could make a difference so that with help and support Tom makes positive choices.

CASE STUDY: TOM'S LIFE

Tom is 15 years old and has been in foster care on and off for most of his life. He has little contact with his mum and hasn't seen his dad in over five years following a huge family row. His current foster placement has resulted in a school move, his third in three years, and if he's honest, he feels lonely and a little out of place amongst his new peers.

Although he is not a gang member he knows some of the boys on his estate are. Watching a TV documentary, *Gangs: The Real Truth*,[2] he is impressed with the loyalty and respect shown by gang members to each other. He hears them call each other 'family' and likes the idea of being part of a family that sticks together and doesn't let you down.

Then he hears the TV presenter interview a local councillor about gangs and youth crime in his area. The councillor seems to really dislike the gangs, saying: 'They are all the same, causing trouble on our streets. The law should punish them hard to give the clear message that we are not prepared to be scared in our own communities.'

Tom feels confused; this is not his experience with the gang members he knows.

---

2   Please note that this is a made up name for the purposes of the scenario. Any similarity with any other TV programme about gang life is purely coincidental.

ACTIVITY 39: CHILD CRIMINAL EXPLOITATION

Aims

- To understand what constitutes child criminal exploitation (CCE).
- To raise awareness about peer grooming.
- To explore how young people can be coerced by peers into criminal activity.

Time: 90 minutes

Key vocabulary

- Child criminal exploitation (CCE)
- Gang
- Peer grooming
- Crime

You will need

- A3 paper and marker pens

How to do it

1. Divide the main group into groups of four and give a sheet of A3 paper and marker pens to each group. Ask them to fold it into eight sections and then number each sections 1–8.

2. Explain that you are going to tell them about the experiences of Billy, a 14-year-old young man recently arrested for gang-related crime. Make it clear that whilst this is not a true story it is a case study put together from the collective experiences of several young men with life experiences like Billy.

3. Read aloud each part of the case study, pausing after each to set a 5-minute discussion-based group task. The outcomes of the task can recorded onto the eight sections of the A3 paper either in words or as a series of pictures.

4. After each task, stop, and invite each group to share their findings, raise points and ask questions. Encourage discussion, especially where this is a difference of opinion, before moving on to the next part.

Case study: Billy

PART 1

Billy is 14 and goes to the local secondary school after moving to a new area with his mum, new stepdad and baby brother a year ago. At his last school he had a good circle of friends he'd known since primary school, but here he struggles to fit in. Everything is different, from the size of the classes and the huge school building to the music and fashions. Even the local football team that the students support is different. The worst thing is that everyone seems to already belong to a friendship group, leaving no room for newcomers. He sometimes wonders if anyone even notices he is there and this is the same at home where his mum seems to be more interested in whatever the baby is doing or spending 'couple time' with his stepdad.

Billy hates it. If he had his way he would go back to live with his dad in their old house, but this doesn't seem to be an option as his dad says he works away too much to look after him. The only part of the day he enjoys is on social media talking to his old friends or gaming, which he does until late at night in his bedroom.

Square 1 task: Discuss the positives and negatives of moving to a new area and then draw or write how Billy might be feeling.

PART 2

As time goes on Billy's feelings of isolation start to change and he now feels angry all the time. It seems that whatever he does is not good enough at home and he has stopped trying to get his mum's attention. She says he is being selfish and that at his age he should know better and realize that she has to spend more time with his brother because he is only a toddler. He did try to talk to his dad about it but was told to 'man up' and stop moaning. Since then he has refused to go for contact with his dad.

Square 2 task: Billy's mum says 'at his age he should know better' – what do you think she means by this? Is she being fair? Ask each group to have a short discussion to consider age-appropriate roles and responsibilities within a family, and then ask them to write key points in square 2.

Square 3 task: When Billy's dad tells him to 'man up', what do you think he means? Ask the young people to identify male stereotypes and then discuss where they see stereotypes of masculinity perpetuated. Ideas can be written in square 3.

PART 3

Billy blames his stepdad for everything. If he hadn't come into their lives his mum and dad would never have split up and they wouldn't have had to move away from all of his friends. Their relationship is now so bad that they can hardly talk without arguing and the silence feels toxic, with unspoken resentment on both sides.

Matters come to a head when his mum confiscates his phone for being rude to his stepdad and after a massive row Billy storms out.

Square 4 task: Is Billy right to blame his stepdad? Who has the responsibility to try to make the relationships at home more positive? What could they all do to make living together work better? Again, record ideas to share later.

PART 4

After the argument with his mum Billy goes to the children's playground, which is somewhere local teenagers often hang out. He can't talk to his usual friends as he has no phone and doesn't want to be on his own with his head filled to bursting with rage at the injustice of it all.

Whilst there, he notices a group of older lads walk past. He doesn't know them by name but he has seen them around and heard people say they are 'trouble'. Normally he would have looked away when they stop and stare at him, just in case, but tonight he is so angry that he stares right back. To his surprise they stop and before long he is laughing and joking with them. When they tell him to be there the next night, he agrees. It's really nice to feel normal again.

Square 5 task: Why do you think Billy usually ignores the older group? What might be his fears and concerns? Is he right to be cautious? How much attention should we pay to gossip about other people?

Square 6 task: Ask the groups to consider the specific circumstances leading up to Billy's decision to make eye contact with the older group. What was different about that night? How might his emotional state have impacted on the decisions he made? Why do you think they decided to befriend him rather than respond to the silent challenge his stare could have presented? What else could have happened?

PART 5

Weeks later and Billy is regularly missing school and has stopped messaging his old friends. He stays away from home more and more, spending most of his time with the older group and coming in only to change his clothes and grab something to eat. Billy's mum complains that he treats the place like a hotel but this masks the fact that she is worried because he refuses to say where he is or who he's with. This makes her short-tempered with his stepdad, who she accuses of not caring. Whilst this is not strictly true, his stepdad is finding it hard not to show that he is secretly grateful for the peace and quiet Billy's absence offers. This leads to arguments between the couple, which in turn unsettles their youngest child who picks up on their moods.

You can almost feel the tension in the house as the arguments rage and accusations fly. Billy doesn't care; he has finally found somewhere he belongs and is enjoying himself. As far as he is concerned, his mum and stepdad deserve all they get.

Square 7 task: Billy's mum is worried about Billy being out and about on his own, especially at night. What might she be worried about? Are her fears realistic? How do these fears compare with those Billy had about the older lads before he got talking to them?

PART 6
Last weekend Billy was reported missing overnight by his mum and the police discovered him, along with some other boys, at a suspected drug dealer's flat on an estate about 10 miles from home. Billy refuses to say how he got there, what he was doing or how he knows the tenant of the flat. On searching him, the police found £350 in cash and a bag of cocaine wraps.

At the police station Billy's mum, dad and stepdad are in shock. Billy has been arrested for drug offences and is suspected of further gang-related crime. 'How did this happen?' they ask the custody sergeant. The custody sergeant says he thinks that Billy has been groomed for child criminal exploitation (CCE).

Square 8 task: What do you think has happened? Is Billy responsible for the choices he made? The custody sergeant says he thinks Billy has been 'groomed' and talks about 'CCE' – what do you think he means? Write group ideas in square 8.

5. After facilitating feedback for the final task, talk more about grooming and CCE:

   - Grooming is when someone deliberately builds an emotional connection with a child to gain their trust for the purposes of exploitation. Children and young people can be groomed online or face-to-face, by a stranger or by someone they know (e.g. a family member, friend or professional).

   - Child criminal exploitation (CCE) is child abuse where children and young people are manipulated and coerced into committing crimes.[3]

6. Acknowledge that Billy has broken the law but ask the young people to consider if they think Billy is a victim or a perpetrator of crime. Point out it is possible to be both, and ask them to consider the likelihood that in time Billy would start to recruit younger gang members.

   Make the point that peer grooming is common and challenge the notion that it is only older men who groom young people to join gangs or participate in gang-related crime.

   According to Knowsley Council, Merseyside: 'perpetrators of CCE may themselves be children who are criminally exploited and victims of CCE may also be at risk of becoming perpetrators themselves.'[4]

7. Facilitate a short whole-group discussion to consolidate learning:

   - What made Billy vulnerable to grooming? *For example, he was lonely; didn't feel he belonged at school; was having difficulties at home; lacked a positive male role model; wasn't engaged in any positive out-of-school activities etc.*

   - What did membership of the gang offer him? *For example, identity; friendship; a sense of belonging; something to do; respect; opportunities to make money etc.*

---

3   See www.nspcc.org.uk/what-is-child-abuse/types-of-abuse/gangs-criminal-exploitation
4   www.knowsley.gov.uk

- What could his (a) mum, (b) dad, (c) stepdad and (d) teachers have done to reduce the likelihood of him getting involved with a gang? *For example, noticed that he was struggling; found time to talk and listen to him; helped him to find positive things to do both in and out of school; helped him make new friends or keep in touch with his old friends etc.*

- What could he have done to keep himself safe? *For example, thought through the potential consequences of his choices; walked away early on; nodded to the older group but not engaged them in conversation etc.*

- What positive steps can he take now? *For example, accept any help offered; talk to the police; build confidence and assertiveness skills; engage in counselling or mediation services to rebuild his family relationships; reconnect with his positive friendship group etc.*

ACTIVITY 40: COUNTY LINES

Aims

- To better understand what is meant by the term 'county lines'.
- To consider the impact that poor choices can have on family, friends and the wider community.
- To explore the potential short- and longer-term consequences of choices made.

Time: 90–120 minutes

Key vocabulary

- 'County lines'
- Vulnerable
- Exploited
- Choice and consequences
- Positive role model

You will need

- Flipchart paper and marker pens
- A4 paper and pens
- Internet access
- Film: *Trapped – County Lines (8.28 minutes)*[5]

How to do it

1. Ask if anyone knows what the term 'county lines' means and listen to responses to assess levels of knowledge and understanding within the group.

   Definition: *County lines* is a criminal strategy first identified in 2014. It describes the approach taken by gangs originating from large urban areas, including London and Manchester, who travel to locations in county or coastal towns to sell class 'A' drugs, which includes reports of towns in Hertfordshire. Gangs typically recruit and exploit children and vulnerable young people to courier drugs and cash as they are less likely to be suspected of breaking the law and the real criminals can remain anonymous. They also use local properties as a base for their activities, and this often involves taking over the home of a vulnerable adult, for example care leavers, young parents and those with disabilities who can feel unable to challenge them. This is known as 'cuckooing'. It is reported that the name 'county lines' refers to a single phone number used to order drugs, which is operated outside of the area, making it harder to trace those responsible.[6]

2. Ask each young person to share an experience of being asked to do something they did not want to do with the person sitting next to them. This could be at home/school/college or something that happened within a friendship group.

   For each example, encourage each young person to explain to the **person next to them** why they didn't want to do it, how it felt to be asked and the tactics the person asking used to try to persuade them, especially if it became clear they didn't really want to say yes.

---

5   www.youtube.com/watch?v=pLhGpS1f-F0
6   For more information, go to the Youth Justice Resource Hub at https://yjresourcehub.uk

Persuasion tactics could include:

- asking nicely

- gentle persuasion

- repeating the request until the person gives in

- emotional blackmail

- bullying

- bribery

- telling them they will be in trouble if they don't

- offering a reward

- threatening to withhold friendship/love

- coercion

- threats of violence.

3. Write in one column on flipchart paper the name of the task and in another the methods of persuasion used. Once everyone has contributed, go back to the list and ask the young people to score each persuasion tactic as acceptable, 'A' or unacceptable, 'U'. Review and compare answers, and ask: What are the 'drivers', that is, the things that make it more likely that someone will say yes? Examples include:

- personal gain

- loyalty

- friendship

- to belong/fit in with a group

- to be loved

- to be admired

- to be left alone.

Suggest that these are all powerful drivers that can be used in both positive and negative ways.

Ask: If you give in and say yes, does it make it harder to say no next time? Why or why not?

4. Move on to look at more serious examples of someone going along with something they later regret. This could include gang crime and county lines.

5. Conclude that there are many different forms of persuasion and that it is not always easy to say no, especially if you like or respect the other person. This can be even harder in situations where not complying could result in threats or violence.

6. Divide the young people into three groups and give out paper and pens and allocate them a different character to focus on. These are:

- the young man

- his girlfriend

- his mother.

Show the film *Trapped – County Lines*. As they watch the film each group should make notes on what they see from the perspective of their allocated character on the following:

- What were the risk factors that made this character vulnerable?

- What positives did they have in their life?

    –   At what point did things change for them?

    –   They all say they had 'no choice'. Do you think this is true? How or why?

Point out that although the film is just a story it does demonstrate how choices made by one person can go on to affect *everyone* around them.

7.   Back in their small groups ask the young people to think of more positive choices that:

    –   the young man could have made

    –   his girlfriend could have made

    –   his mother could have made.

8.   Then ask them to mind map the likely consequences of these to a conclusion where the young man and his family are able to start again, free of gang involvement. This might not be an easy task, so allow as much time as required to resolve the situation.

If someone is concerned about or has information about 'county lines' they can report it directly to the police or anonymously to Crime Stoppers by calling 0800 555 111 or they can go online and complete and submit an anonymous form.[7]

---

7   The form can be found at https://crimestoppers-uk.org/give-information/forms/give-information-anonymously

ACTIVITY 41: JOINT ENTERPRISE

Aims

- To better understand the meaning of 'joint enterprise'.
- To explore concepts of blame and responsibility, legal and otherwise.

Time: 60 minutes

Key vocabulary

- Joint enterprise law
- Peer pressure
- Violent crime
- Knives
- Consequences

You will need

- Copies of the Joint Enterprise Consequences cards (cut up)
- Flipchart paper and marker pens

How to do it

1. Ask: Who has heard the old saying 'birds of a feather flock together'?

    Invite the young people to call out what they think it means before moving on to consider how true it is. Suggest that whilst people can and do retain their individuality within groups, there is some truth in the idea that those with shared interests, values, experiences and ideals do tend to find each other, both in real life and online. Test this by asking the young people how many of them have friends they have nothing in common with. Then ask for examples of friendships with others who share interests, which could include online forums, political parties, faith groups, community groups, supporters of a specific football team or followers of a particular social media influencer.

    Ask: When might this assumption become problematic? Answers could include:

    - assumptions that lead to negative stereotypes, *for example, all young people belong to gangs or commit crime etc.*
    - assumptions of guilt by association, *for example, you know people who commit crimes so you must be a criminal too*
    - assumptions that everyone who likes one thing dislikes people who like something else, *for example, if you all your friends live in one area you must hate anyone who lives in the next postcode.*

2. Divide the young people into a maximum of five small groups. They will stay in this group for the rest of the exercise.

    Read aloud the 'Joint enterprise scenario' at least once to ensure everyone hears and understands it.

3. Next give each group a sheet of flipchart paper, marker pens and one of the five Joint Enterprise Consequences. Allow time for each group to read and digest the scenario they have been allocated. These should not be shared with other groups at this point.

4. Whilst they do this, write the first task, which refers directly to the scenario, on a sheet of flipchart paper and display it where everyone can see it:

    Task One

    - Is Dante right to blame himself? How or why?

    - How responsible is he for the stabbing? How or why?

    - Who else is responsible for what happened? How or why?

5. Invite each group to read out the Joint Enterprise Consequences they were given and then present back their work on Task One. Encourage debate and facilitate any differences of opinions so that all perspectives are heard.

6. Back in their groups, set Task Two:

    Task Two

    - What do you think should happen now? Consider this from the perspective of all those involved.

7. Allow 10 minutes for discussion and then ask for feedback. These are likely to include arrest, interview and intelligence gathering as well as practical things like the police visiting the victim's family to break the bad news.

8. Introduce the concept of 'joint enterprise'. This means that if you are with someone who commits a crime or your actions lead to a crime being committed you could be charged with the same offence as the main offender if it can be proved that you knew what was going to happen. For example, if a young person encourages or enables a fellow gang member to commit a knife attack where the victim later dies, they, too, could be charged with murder.

    In the Dante/Ryan scenario the joint enterprise law could apply to Dante because he took a knife to a fight where he expected violence, even though the knife was not his and he did not use it.

    It's important that the young people know that if a crime is committed, by being there they could have some culpability. Encourage them to:

    -   recognize when a situation is dangerous

    -   make assertive decisions about not carrying a weapon and stick to them

    -   report it if they think a serious crime is about to be committed

    -   make positive choices.

    Fact: The vast majority of young people don't carry a knife.

    Fact: The consequences of carrying a knife can be four years in prison, even if it's never used.

    Fact: If you carry a knife and use it, even in self-defence, you could be convicted with aggravated assault, attempted murder/murder or manslaughter, which could carry a life sentence.

    Fact: There is an increased risk of receiving a violence-related injury if you carry a knife, for example, if the knife is taken off you and used against you.

9. Finally, suggest that the choice Dante made to take a knife out that evening will be a life-changing experience for everyone involved. Wordstorm some of the potential long-term negative consequences from the viewpoints of different characters. These could include:

    -   Dante serving a long sentence for murder if joint enterprise is proved in court

    -   his own mental health, for example, post-traumatic stress disorder following the violence he witnessed, recurring guilt and remorse

    -   impact on his educational opportunities, for example, school exclusion, not being able to get into the university of his choice

- travel limitations, for example, not being allowed into some countries because of his criminal record

- social isolation, for example, rejection from peers, friends disassociating themselves

- trauma and grief for the families of all those involved: the bereaved family of the victim, Dante's family, the family of the person who used the knife who will struggle to come to terms with the knowledge that their child took the life of another etc.

- emotional and social damage done to the community, for example, grief at the loss of life and violence, residents feeling unsafe and/or scared to go out, parents fearing that other children living there will join a gang, fear of retaliation, the negative reputation of the community etc.

10. Direct the young people online to learn about a real-life example. Ben Kinsella was stabbed to death in Islington, London by three youths in 2008.[8]

11. Conclude that the consequences of choosing to carry a knife can be far-reaching and impact on your life forever. That's why it is important to know the facts and to make the decision to be knife-free.

Joint enterprise scenario: Ryan and Dante

Ryan and Dante are members of the same gang currently at war with another youth gang in the area. Ryan is older than Dante and has been like a mentor to him since he joined, always taking the time to talk to him and helping him fit in.

Tonight there is a planned meet between the two rival gangs. Dante knows it is likely to turn violent and is feeling a mixture of fear and excitement. At 12 years old it will be the first time that he's been involved with anything like this. Adrenaline is pumping as the time gets closer, and when Ryan turns up early at his door and asks him to conceal a knife, he feels responsible and proud.

Fast-forward a couple of hours and Dante's excitement has turned to shock and terror at what he witnessed. Sitting in the back of a police car, he can't help but wish he'd stayed home because tonight someone was stabbed with the knife that Ryan asked Dante to carry. He never realized how much blood was in a person or how the smell of warm blood would stick in his nose and the sound of pain would replay in his brain.

'I may not have stabbed anyone', thinks Dante, 'but it wouldn't have happened if I hadn't agreed to carry the knife.'

Suddenly he feels very young and alone.

---

8   To read about his sister's life, which has been changed forever, see Shute, J. (2018) 'Brooke Kinsella: "Ten years after my brother was stabbed to death, I'm too scared to have children."' *The Telegraph*, 13 April. Available at www.telegraph.co.uk/women/life/brooke-kinsella-10-years-losing-brother-ben-cant-stop-rising

JOINT ENTERPRISE CONSEQUENCES

Group 1: Later that night a 16-year-old boy from the rival gang dies in hospital. The knife severed an artery in his left leg and he died without regaining consciousness.

Group 2: Paramedics pronounce Ryan dead at the scene. The knife was dropped in the fight and a member of the rival gang stabbed him with it. His attacker punctured a lung and Ryan drowned in his own blood.

Group 3: Dante discovers the stab victim was a 45-year-old father of three trying to help another boy injured in the fight. Two of the man's fingers were severed when he raised his hands to protect his face.

Group 4: The person screaming was a 16-year-old girl, the girlfriend of one of the gang members. An aspiring model and Instagram influencer, she lost an eye when she was sliced across her face with the knife.

Group 5: At the police station Dante is told that the person stabbed was an off-duty police officer that tried to break up the fight before it escalated. A young mother, the police officer, is currently fighting for her life after receiving six stab wounds.

ACTIVITY 42: JOINT ENTERPRISE – FOR AND AGAINST

Aims

- To research a true case of joint enterprise to see what can be learned from the past.
- To discuss the legal dilemmas that joint enterprise law presents.

Time: 90 minutes

Key vocabulary

- Joint enterprise law
- Crime
- Weapon
- Law
- Consequences

You will need

- Internet access for research
- Paper and pens

Facilitator note: Research online the historic joint enterprise case of Derek Bentley[9] in advance. Refer to the briefing notes provided.

How to do it

1. Start by facilitating a short voting activity using the questions below to explore personal attitudes and values. Do this by reading out the questions and then asking the young people to vote 'yes' or 'no' by raising their right hand for 'yes' or keeping both arms down for 'no'.

2. After each vote facilitate a short discussion to consider different points of view. Note that the answers are opinion-based so there is no 'right' answer, although it should be reinforced throughout that in the UK it is illegal to carry a weapon and commit violent crime.

   - Is it human nature to sort out disagreements by fighting?
   - Is there such a thing as a 'fair fight'?
   - Is everyone who carries a weapon potentially capable of violence?
   - If you choose to carry a knife, should you be prepared to use it?
   - Should people who choose to carry a weapon expect to face the full force of the law if they get caught?
   - If you knowingly go out with people who carry knives, are you as responsible as them for anything that happens?

3. Divide the young people into groups of four. Explain that you are going to explore the issues raised about joint culpability in the last question by researching a true crime. The case involves a young man called Derek Bentley, who was convicted of murder after his accomplice in a burglary, Christopher Craig, shot a police officer dead.

---

9   http://news.bbc.co.uk/onthisday/hi/dates/stories/january/28/newsid_3393000/3393807.stm

DEREK BENTLEY BRIEFING NOTES

- In 1953, Derek Bentley (aged 19) was hanged for his part in the murder of a police officer, Sidney Miles.

- PC Sidney Miles was shot dead after he and other officers caught two young men attempting to break into a warehouse in Croydon.

- Derek did take a weapon with him that knight, a 'knuckle duster', which he did not use.

- There was only one gun, which belonged to Derek's accomplice, Christopher ('Chris') Craig.

- Chris fired the shots, wounding one police officer and killing another.

- Derek's conviction hinged on police evidence that he allegedly said 'Let him have it, Chris', which the prosecution said instructed Chris Craig to fire.

- Derek's barrister argued that when he said 'Let him have it, Chris' he was actually instructing his friend to surrender the gun to the police.

- Because Chris was only 16 (a child in the eyes of the law) he was convicted of murder but escaped the death sentence and being sent to prison.

- Although he was older than Chris, the defence argued that Derek, who had epilepsy and learning disabilities, was not the ringleader. Despite this he was convicted of murder using the joint enterprise law.

- There was much opposition to the death penalty being carried out, and up until the last moments supporters, including Derek's family, were hoping for a reprieve.

- This didn't happen and Derek was hung at Wandsworth Jail on 28 January 1953.

What happened next?

Christopher Craig served 10 years in prison and was then released. Campaigns for justice for Derek, led by his family, were partially successful in 1993 when the then Home Secretary Michael Howard granted Bentley a partial pardon, saying it was clear he should never have been hanged but he remained guilty of taking part in the murder. In 1998 the Appeal Court quashed Derek Bentley's conviction on the grounds the original trial judge was biased against the defendants and misdirected the jury on points of law. At that point Derek Bentley had been dead for 45 years.

Lessons learned?

Derek Bentley was one of the last men in Britain to be sentenced to the death penalty, and outrage over the case contributed to its abolishment. It remains one of the most infamous examples of the use of joint enterprise law. Although his conviction was eventually quashed in 1998 after years of campaigning, neither his father nor his sister lived long enough to see his pardon.

ACTIVITY 43: CHILD SEXUAL EXPLOITATION

Aims

- To recognize the vulnerabilities that make a young person more at risk of sexual grooming.
- To introduce the 'relationship model' of child sexual exploitation (CSE).
- To understand how young people can be targeted and groomed for sexual exploitation.

Time: 90–120 minutes

Key vocabulary

- Child sexual exploitation (CSE)
- Control and coercion
- Vulnerable
- Exploited

You will need

- Flipchart paper or a whiteboard and marker pens
- Sticky tack
- Paper and pens
- Copies of the Trust Me worksheet
- A copy of the messages scenarios
- Social media platforms to reinforce positive relationship messages and raise awareness about CSE at different points in the session (optional)

Facilitator notes: Research child sexual abuse campaigner, Sammy Woodhouse,[10] who was the first young woman to blow the whistle on a paedophile ring grooming and sexually abusing girls and young women in Rotherham. This triggered the Jay Report,[11] which exposed 1400 children abused and failed in Rotherham.

How to do it

1. Draw a large heart shape in the middle of a sheet of flipchart paper or on a whiteboard. Then ask the young people to call out the things that they believe make a positive relationship. Write ideas inside the heart shape in different-coloured pens, explaining that these are blending together to create a 'love heart'. Make sure that 'trust' is identified as a major component in a healthy, positive relationship.

2. Once complete, display on a wall to refer to later. Consider posting the picture on social media with appropriate hashtags, for example, #positiverelationships #loveislove etc. to share with other young people.

3. Next, working in pairs, ask the young people to think about the people closest to them, those they really like/love, respect and trust, and then to come up with six skills or qualities that they think make someone trustworthy.

4. Bring everyone together to draw a collective list of suggestions. These could include:

---

10 https://sammywoodhouse.com/my-story
11 www.rotherham.gov.uk/downloads/download/31/independent-inquiry-into-child-sexual-exploitation-in-rotherham-1997---2013

- honesty

- mutual respect

- good listeners

- dependable

- understanding

- ability to see things from different points of view

- ability to positively challenge

- doing what they say they will

- believing they have your best interests at heart.

Ask: How do you know you can trust someone when you first meet them?

Take suggestions, but point out that real trust is built up over time and that it is impossible to know if someone is being honest on a first meeting. This doesn't mean we should be suspicious of everyone new we meet, just that it is better to get to know someone slowly and let the relationship develop gradually before sharing personal information and intimate details. This is especially important online.

5. Read 'Sophie's story' out loud and then distribute the Trust Me worksheet and pens. Explain that Meg is right to be concerned because behind AJ's loving 'boyfriend' façade he is trying to manipulate and control her. Tell them that the sentences on the worksheet have come from messages sent by AJ to Sophie via text and social media, and that they will later be used by the police as evidence that he was grooming her. Point out that at the time Sophie received the messages she believed she was in a loving, consensual relationship and had no idea that she was about to become a victim of CSE.

NSPCC[12] definitions of 'child' and 'CSE':

- Child = someone under the age of 18.

- Child sexual exploitation (CSE) is a type of sexual abuse. When a child or young person is exploited they're given things, like gifts, drugs, money, status and affection, in exchange for performing sexual activities. Children and young people are often tricked into believing they're in a loving and consensual relationship. This is called grooming. They may trust their abuser and not understand that they're being abused.

6. Now that they have the facts, ask the young people to work in pairs to review what AJ says and then consider what they think the meaning or intention is behind it. They can write their ideas in the second column on the Trust Me worksheet.

7. Allow 15 minutes and then, taking it in turns, invite each pair to offer suggestions on the different things AJ has said. Encourage discussion where there is more than one meaning identified, especially as on the face of it not everything he said has a potentially sinister meaning.

8. Go back to the list originally generated about the meaning of trust. Ask: Based on this, should Sophie place her trust in AJ? *Explore the reasons for and against.*

9. Remind the young people that at this point Sophie has not questioned AJ's motive and continues to believe that her feelings of love and admiration are reciprocated. Divide the young people into three groups, furnishing each with large sheets of paper and pens. Allocate the messages scenarios one to each group:

- Group 1: Sophie's message

---

12   www.nspcc.org.uk/what-is-child-abuse/types-of-abuse/child-sexual-exploitation

- Group 2: Meg's message

- Group 3: AJ's message

Explain that each message contains the thoughts and feelings of a character. Their task is to consider the choices available to that character based on the information they have, and then to identify the likely consequences of each one. This should be done using a 'mind map' technique, where they put the scenario in the middle and then explore the different things that the character could say or do using pictures, arrows and text boxes. At the end they should draw a thick border around the choice that they think will give the most positive outcome to keep both young women safe. Suggest that mind mapping is a good technique to use when there is more than one potential solution.

10. Allow up to 20 minutes for this task to be completed and then draw everyone back together. Invite each group to present:

    - the scenario they have been working on

    - the choices that could be made, with a brief synopsis of the likely consequences, ending with the choice they think should be made and the reasons why.

    Explain that like Sophie, some young people are groomed using a 'relationship model'. They can later be coerced or controlled into carrying weapons and drugs for a gang, used to entrap rival gang members, as rewards for elders in a gang, and/or shared to pay off drug debts, all of which puts them at risk of violence and sexual violence.

11. Using this 'relationship model' of CSE, ask the young people to suggest some examples where it might be hard to refuse to do what is asked of you, even if you don't want to. Answers could include:

    - The person asking is someone you like or love.

    - You feel too embarrassed to say no.

    - You are frightened or worried about what will happen to yourself or others if you say no.

    - You think you will look silly by refusing.

12. Go back to the 'love heart' that was created at the start of the session to compare and contrast the indicators of healthy, positive relationships with AJ's words, thoughts and actions. Stress that in real life any child could be targeted for CSE no matter their age, gender, sexual orientation or race, but ask for suggestions as to why they think that Sophie was vulnerable to this type of grooming. This could include:

    - feeling unloved and unwanted by her parents

    - her parents being too preoccupied to keep an eye on her

    - lack of parental boundaries

    - feeling isolated and lonely

    - wanting positive attention

    - feeling flattered by the attention of an older male

    - thinking she had found someone she could trust.

    Remark that having wealthy parents did not make a difference to Sophie and that this can be true in real life too. Whilst stereotypes might point towards children in care, those living in insecure housing, poverty or areas of deprivation, it is important to realize that seemingly rich children, with lots of material goods, can be lacking affection, love and attention, making them vulnerable to predators too. Equally, perpetrators of grooming and CSE come from diverse backgrounds and can be any age.

13. Back working in pairs, direct the young people to carry out a 20-minute online search for Sammy Woodhouse. They should find out as much as they can about Sammy, her childhood experiences,

the impact CSE has had on her life and that of her family, and what she does now. Instruct them to note down their findings to share later.

Facilitator note: Sammy Woodhouse is a child abuse survivor who exposed the biggest child abuse scandal in British history in Rotherham. She has written a book, *Just a Child*,[13] which details her teenage experiences of being groomed and abused by an older man she believed to be her boyfriend. She now works as a public speaker, campaigner and fundraiser to raise awareness about CSE and fights for better joined-up working by the police, social care, education and other public services to better protect and support vulnerable children.

14. Call time and invite each pair to present key points from their research. Encourage conversations to explore the failings in the support that Sammy received as identified in the Jay Report, how she overcame adversity and how the work she does now contributes to making things better for other children and young people. This could include newspaper reports, extracts from her book, threads from her social media accounts, which are part of her campaigning, and videos of her describing her experiences. They could also look at the Sammy Woodhouse Twitter campaign, @sammywoodhouse1

15. Finally, ask the young people if they know of local and national sources of support and help for young people at risk of, or victims of, CSE. Encourage them to share knowledge and understanding of what different organizations offer. These should include:

   – Childline

   – Barnardo's

   – NSPCC

   – Women's Aid (domestic abuse support for females)

   – Respect (domestic abuse support for male victims and perpetrators)

   – Galop (LGBT+ anti-violence charity)

   – Child Exploitation and Online Protection Centre (CEOP).

Sophie's story

Sophie is 15 years old and lives in a big house with her mum and dad. On the surface she has everything anyone could ever want: a massive bedroom with an en suite and a 72" TV; she goes on holiday three times a year to amazing places; she has a pony of her own and has been promised a brand new BMW for her 18th birthday. Everyone tells her how lucky she is that her parents are rich, but things aren't quite as they seem. Behind closed doors her mum and dad row all the time over her dad's affairs and her mum copes by drinking herself unconscious most nights. Sophie spends the majority of her time outside of school online in her bedroom with her headphones firmly on to block out the latest argument.

That is until she met the one person in the world who seems to understand what she is going through. His name is AJ and they met after he DM'd her on social media. He may be older and their lives may be different but in every other way they share so much. He, too, had problems at home but found support amongst his friends. When he talks about belonging and the loyalty and respect they show each other, she knows she would give up everything to be part of it in a heartbeat.

Confiding in a school friend Sophie is shocked when Meg warns her off, telling her she must be mad to get involved with AJ. Meg says AJ is an elder in a local gang and that the lovely AJ Sophie knows is just a mask because the man behind it is nothing like that.

Sophie feels angry and betrayed – how could Meg be like this? Her friend must be wrong, that, or she is jealous. AJ is so kind and thoughtful; he has been completely honest about his past and she trusts him completely. He can't be in a gang or any of the horrid things that Meg says because he treats her like a princess and she's proud to be his girl.

---

13   Available at bookshops, including www.waterstones.com/book/just-a-child/sammy-woodhouse/9781788700078

TRUST ME

What AJ says	Why he says it
No one understands you like I do	
I like it best when there is just you and me	
It's dangerous out there but you have me to keep you safe	
Other people are just jealous of the love we have	
You are special to me	
I go crazy when I'm not with you	
Your family make me feel uncomfortable	
If your friends cared they would accept me	
You are more mature than your friends, they seem like kids	
You don't need anyone else now you have me	
This can be our secret	
I like to know where you are at all times	
You make me a better person	
Wear this, I like you looking sexy	
I want you all to myself	
I only get angry because I love you so much	
I wouldn't want to live without you	
If you love me you will do what I ask	
Only you can help me get out of danger	
It's only the once	

Sophie's message to Meg

Things are going so well with AJ. I just wish you could see us together and you'd realize how good he is for me. It's not just the little gifts he buys that make me feel so special. Last night he drove us all the way to his friend's chicken shop just because I wanted a takeaway. How amazing is that? It was great to meet everyone and see the respect his friends have for him; nothing was too much trouble and I was treated like a princess.

We're planning a future together and I can't wait to be with AJ all the time. I already see him most nights; my parents haven't even noticed I'm never home. It is so good to be with someone who wants me. He says there is nothing he wouldn't do to protect me, and I believe him.

The only downside is arguing with you. You're my best friend and I don't want to lose you but AJ says that if you can't be happy for us then I should cut you out of my life. I guess that it's up to you now. xxx

Meg's message to Sophie

I'm glad you are happy. You're my best friend and I want nothing but good things for you but I miss us spending time together and don't understand why AJ doesn't like you coming out with your friends anymore. I know you said being with him makes you realize how immature the boys our age are, but surely there is enough room in your life for all of us?

I wasn't being horrible when I told you what I've heard about him, I am genuinely worried. I've heard that he deals drugs and has been in trouble with the police. He also has a reputation for going out with younger girls and treating them badly and I don't want this to happen to you.

I know you think I'm jealous and part of me is. I feel like he has stolen my best friend and I wish things could go back to how they were before you met him. He's no good for you, I just wish you could see it. xxx

AJ's message to his friend

She's young, she's sweet and she totally loves me – in fact I think she'd do anything I ask, which is perfect really. Will send you pics from last night so you can see what I mean. What is it with rich girls that make them so hot for bad boys? Not complaining, just sayin

She has this friend Meg that might be right for you? Cute and young looking, just like you love 'em. At the moment Meg hates me for taking away her little friend blah blah but I'm sure if anyone can change her mind you can. Same old trick – tell her she's beautiful, get her talking and before you know it she's yours! Might have to buy a few vodkas and take her out in the car to keep her happy but I'll put in a good word with Sophie. We're gonna need a few girls to get business done so let's put the work in now.

Bring it on

ACTIVITY 44: CARRYING A KNIFE: PERCEPTIONS AND REALITY

Aim

- To explore perceptions about the number of people who choose to carry a knife and to challenge any misconceptions.

Time: 45 minutes

Key vocabulary

- Crime
- Weapon
- Knife
- Perceptions
- Consequences

You will need

- Sticky notes (in three different colours)
- Large sheets of paper and pens
- A selection of newspaper reports on knife crime – from a range of different tabloid papers and broadsheets across the political landscape

How to do it

1. Ask: Why might someone choose to carry a weapon? Answers could include for protection, as a deterrent, to fit in, fear, scare tactics etc.

2. Give each young person three sticky notes and a pen. Ask them to number the sticky notes 1–3. Then ask them to write down the three weapons that they think are the most popular with young people, with '1' being most popular and '3' less so.

3. Once they have done this, direct the young people to stick them on the wall in designated zones 1, 2 and 3. This will provide a visual representation of the weapons considered most popular within the group, which tends to be knives.

4. Divide the young people into small groups, give them flipchart paper and pens, and ask them to discuss and make notes on the following questions:

   - What evidence did you base your suggestions on for the most popular weapons?

   - Where did you get your information?

5. Invite feedback from each group, recording suggestions about sources of information. These could include word of mouth, TV, newspapers, online etc.

6. Back in their groups, give out the newspaper reports you have collected. This time ask each group to discuss how they think the language used, pictures and information in the knife crime reports might impact on a young person considering carrying a knife for the first time.

Ideas should be written under two headings: 'Make it more likely' and 'Make it less likely'. For example:

Make it more likely	Make it less likely
They think everyone carries a knife	They realize the damage knives do to lives
They perceive that everywhere is dangerous	They know they might go to prison

Suggest that the perception of how many young people carry a knife might not be an accurate reflection of what is really happening. Whilst there appears to be a rise in knife crime in the UK in recent years, not all of it is committed by young people, and researchers say it is difficult to get a truly accurate picture because of changes in the way that crimes have been recorded and classified. One police report states that '99.9% of children and young people across the country do not have knives on them'.[14]

---

14 https://southyorkshire-pcc.gov.uk/blogs/99-9-of-young-people-are-not-carrying-knives

ACTIVITY 45: KNIVES: IT'S YOUR CHOICE

Aims

- To find non-violent strategies to challenge the decision to carry a knife for protection.
- To better understand the risks and potential consequences of carrying a knife.

Time: 45 minutes

Key vocabulary

- Choice
- Knife
- Consequences

You will need

- Copies of the It's Your Choice role-play cards

How to do it

1. Divide the group into pairs. Ask one partner in each pair to raise their hand (left or right, dependent on which is their dominant hand) and then to make a tight fist. The second person now has 1 minute to find ways to open the fist, without aggression or threat of harm.

2. Call time and repeat, this time swapping roles.

3. Again, call time after 1 minute and ask how many people managed to get their partner's fist open. Use a show of hands to assess numbers. Then ask how many people got their partner's fist open without any physical contact. It is likely that the majority of people tried initially to prise their partner's fingers open, whilst being mindful of the rules.

4. Review by asking:

    -   What strategies did they use?

    -   How many simply requested their partner to open their hand?

    -   How acceptable is it to use force to get what you want?

    Suggest that developing the skills for non-violent solutions to challenging situations can reduce the likelihood of a confrontation escalating into violence.

5. Divide the young people into groups of three. Explain that they will each be given a set of role-play cards where one young person has decided to carry a knife for protection and a friend is advising against it. In each example, the task is to find a way to stop them taking it out into the community, without using violence or physical threats.

6. Give out sets of It's Your Choice role-play cards. Participants will take at least one turn to role-play the person with the knife, the person persuading them to re-think and the observer, who will offer feedback on the strategies used afterwards. They will have 3 minutes to try to resolve followed by 1 minute's feedback from the observer before swapping roles.

7. Once all of the scenarios have been explored, bring the whole group back together and discuss:

    -   the most effective arguments for not carrying a knife

    -   the biggest barriers to encouraging someone to reconsider

    -   the most effective ways to encourage positive decision-making.

Point out the following:

- Carrying a knife is illegal and could lead to a custodial sentence.

- If you carry a knife you are much more likely to use it and to get stabbed yourself.

- Statistics show that one in three knife-related injuries are caused by the victim's own knife.

- If you carry a knife and use it, even in self-defence, you could be convicted with aggravated assault, attempted murder/murder or manslaughter, which could carry a life sentence.

A criminal record for carrying a weapon can affect your long- and short-term plans, depending on the crime and the sentence you receive. For example, if you want to go to university or college, some might not accept you with a criminal record. Travel visas to some countries, e.g. US, Australia or Thailand, may be denied and a criminal record for drugs or a violent offence could impact negatively on some career choices. Although some convictions might be 'spent' they won't be wiped clean, and for some jobs you may have to declare them to every potential employer for the rest of your working life.

IT'S YOUR CHOICE

I carry it for protection – it makes me feel safer	No one will start on me if they know I have a knife
Most of my friends carry a knife	I'd only ever use it in self-defence
I wouldn't ever use it, it's just for show	It's only a kitchen knife, not a real weapon
I carry if for my friend as I'm less likely to be arrested	If I got caught I would just tell the police it's for fishing
It's not as bad as carrying a gun	I hide it so well that no one is going to see it
It's to show loyalty to my friends	I have no choice, it's something I have to do

ACTIVITY 46: GUN CRIME

Aims

- To explore feelings and attitudes to firearms.
- To raise awareness about UK gun laws.
- To discuss the potential consequences of carrying a gun.
- To consider the effectiveness of gun amnesties.

Time: 60 minutes

Key vocabulary

- Guns
- Firearms
- Serious Violence Strategy (2018)[15]
- Shooting
- Consequences

You will need

- Film: Metropolitan Police video #GiveUpYourGun, *Carrying a Gun is My Choice*[16]

How to do it

1. Introduce the session by reading out this quote from the head of Scotland Yard's Violent Crime Directorate, Barry Norman:

   Serious youth violence is the biggest problem we have today – with the possible exception of terrorism.[17]

   Ask:

   - Do you agree with him?

   - If you were a young person considering carrying a gun for protection, would it make you more or less likely to get one?

2. Call out the following examples, asking the young people to raise their right hand if they think the gun use described is acceptable and valid and to keep their hands down if they don't. Explain that some raise ethical or political questions where opinion may vary, and encourage discussion where there are differences of opinion:

   - farmers shooting rabbits and other vermin on their land

   - deer stalking weekends on a country estate

   - armed police in a hostage situation

   - soldiers in the army

---

15 www.gov.uk/government/publications/serious-violence-strategy
16 www.youtube.com/watch?time_continue=54&v=a4WPlunq6y0
17 Quoted in Sergeant, H. (2009) 'Feral youths: How a generation of violent, illiterate young men are living outside the boundaries of civilised life.' Mail Online, 19 September. Available at www.dailymail.co.uk/debate/article-1214549/Feral-youths-How-generation-violent-illiterate-young-men-living-outside-boundaries-civilised-society.html

- shooting targets on a firing range

- clay pigeon shooting in a competition.

Ask: What makes these examples of gun use different to guns used in criminal activity or on the streets? This should include:

- having a licence for the gun

- being taught how to shoot

- using the gun legally

- being accountable for shots fired.

Point out that the use of firearms in the UK is tightly controlled by legislation, and that the country has one of the lowest gun homicide rates in the world.

ACTIVITY 47: HELPING A FRIEND

Aim

- To identify ways to help a friend at risk of gang involvement.

Time: 20 minutes

Key vocabulary

- Friendship
- Help
- Support
- Keeping safe

You will need

- Copies of the Case Notes Scenario
- Paper and pens

How to do it

1. Start by suggesting that peers often notice when something isn't right long before adults do, including teachers and parents. However, a combination of not knowing how to help and fear of making things worse can mean that they say nothing.

2. Divide the young people into pairs, giving each couple a Case Notes Scenario, paper and pens. Explain that the scenario depicts the concerns of a young man worried that his friend has got involved in gang-related criminal activity. Unable to talk to anyone else, the young man has contacted a children's charity and spoken to a support worker. The scenario is a summary of the case notes recorded by that worker.

3. Once they have read the scenario, explain that the task for each pair is to draft an email response that will support the worried friend and offer guidance on things he could do to help and what to avoid doing. This can be recorded on the paper.

4. Allow 15 minutes to draft the email and then invite each pair to present their response. Ideas could include:

   - encouraging his friend to talk about it
   - listening carefully to understand what is happening
   - trying not to make a judgement about choices made
   - encouraging his friend to think about their safety
   - not demanding details or confidences that might put him at risk
   - not making promises he can't keep
   - suggesting they get help from a trusted adult and offering to go with him
   - knowing when to break a confidence if his friend is in danger
   - calling the police if danger is imminent.

5. Once all of the ideas have been considered and discussed, move on to consider things to avoid as they could escalate the situation and make matters worse. These could include:

    –   trying to solve the problem alone

    –   going to the gang to 'have it out'

    –   telling lies to cover up what's happening

    –   acting aggressively or making threats

    –   forcing his friend to make choices, for example, his friendship or the gang

    –   telling peers about the situation and gossiping

    –   getting into online trolling or arguments.

    Suggest that sometimes being a true friend can mean having to make difficult choices to keep someone safe. In this example the best thing Liam can do is tell a trusted adult and get the right help and support before things escalate any further.

CASE NOTES SCENARIO

Phone call to: Children's charity

From: Liam (aged 15)

Concerns: Liam contacted us to report concerns he has about gang-related activity.

Summary: Liam is worried about his friend, Matthew, who has been missing a lot of school and refuses to say where he goes or who with. Matthew always has lots of money that he keeps in a moneybag around his waist, but when Liam asked about it, Matthew got angry and told him to mind his own business.

Liam thinks his friend has really changed since he started hanging around with an older group. Individuals in this group are well known to police in the area. Matthew has started smoking cannabis and stopped attending the sports club they both belong to.

After a drug awareness workshop in school, Liam has become convinced that Matthew is dealing for a gang. In the workshop youth workers told pupils about something called 'county lines', where urban gangs recruit young people to travel out of area to sell drugs, using dedicated mobile phones or 'lines'. Liam says this fits with his friend's absences, the extra money and his reluctance to talk about what's happening in his life.

Liam contacted us because he is scared for Matthew and doesn't know what to do.

ACTIVITY 48: BARRIERS TO ACCESSING SUPPORT

Aims

- To identify potential barriers to asking for help.
- To raise awareness about where to go for reliable information and support.

Time: 30 minutes

Key vocabulary

- Barriers
- Help
- Support in staying safe

You will need

- A5 paper and pens
- Flipchart paper and marker pens

How to do it

1. Open the session by posing the question: Why might someone keep gang-related anxieties to themselves?

2. Hand out a piece of A5 paper and a pen to everyone and ask each person to write on one side why someone might not want to ask for help or support if they are worried about gang-related activities and/or crime. This could include:

    - not knowing where to go for support
    - feeling embarrassed or ashamed
    - fear of gang reprisals on self or others
    - family culture of 'keeping quiet'
    - fear of the police
    - knowing they have committed a crime themselves and might face justice
    - not knowing the right time to ask
    - thinking no one else cares
    - believing you should be able to sort it out yourself
    - worrying that it will make things worse.

3. Collect all the papers in and hand them out again at random, this time asking them to write a response on the other side of the paper to challenge the statement and encourage someone to speak up and get help.

4. Collect the papers in and distribute them, again asking each person to read out the one they have been given. Invite discussion and any other suggestions they may have.

5. Divide the young people into two teams and hand each a sheet of flipchart paper and marker pens. Allow 2 minutes for each group to write down as many sources of information, help and support as they can think of. This could include things like websites and online helplines as well

as real-world sources like school, the police, parents, health services etc. Call time and invite each team to share their ideas.

6. Conclude that there is help available for a whole range of gang-related issues and emphasize the importance of asking for support.

7. Still in groups, explain that you are now going to call out a list of gang-related topics that young people might want support with. As you do, each group should go online to identify reliable sources. This can be done using mobile phones, tablets or laptops:

   – bullying

   – sexual health information

   – drug and alcohol support services

   – grooming and child sexual exploitation (CSE)

   – child criminal exploitation (CCE)

   – information about stop and search laws

   – domestic abuse

   – knife crime

   – county lines.

   Point out that whilst there is plenty of information and support available online, some can be wrong, biased, inappropriate or simply the view of one person, so it is important to use a reputable source.

   For additional information and support on gang-related activities and crime, refer them to:

   – #knifefree, for information on how to live knife-free: www.knifefree.co.uk

   – Childline, support and advice for young people about a range of issues: www.childline.org.uk

   – Fearless, advice and a way to anonymously report crime: www.fearless.org

   – Victim Support, support for anyone who has been a victim of crime: www.victimsupport.org.uk

   – The Ben Kinsella Trust: www.benkinsella.org.uk

   – In an emergency, call the police using 999.

   – For a non-emergency phone number, the police can be contacted using 101.

ACTIVITY 49: **REPORT IT**

Aims

- To raise awareness of different types of weapon crime.
- To give information about the government's Serious Violence Strategy (2018).[18]
- To inform young people how and where to report weapon crime.

Time: 45 minutes

Key vocabulary

- Guns
- Firearms
- Serious Violence Strategy (2018)
- Shooting
- Consequences

You will need

- Sets of the Weapon Crime cards

How to do it

1. Divide the young people into groups of four and give each group a set of the Weapon Crime cards. On each card is the outline of a weapon-related offence. The task is to read and discuss each scenario and then place it on a continuum of 'Most likely to report' and 'Least likely to report'. Explain that for each you will be asking one group to share the thinking behind their decision before the rest of the group is invited to comment.

2. Allow up 20 minutes for discussion and then invite feedback from each group, which takes it in turns to take the lead in explaining their decisions about each of the different scenarios.

   - Which crimes are you most likely to report? What would make it more or less likely? *For example, more likely = if you felt someone you knew was at risk; if the threat was applicable to whatever groups you belong to; if it was more likely to result in a death etc. Less likely = if it wasn't something you consider dangerous; if you were not affected; if you were too scared or felt intimidated etc.*

   - What might happen if it is not reported? *For example, it could escalate; it gives the message that it is acceptable; vulnerable young people could be targeted; more people could join in; someone could be harmed or even killed.*

3. Discuss where to report threats of crime:

   - Online threats, images of illegal activity etc. should be reported to the service provider.

   - If you think that someone you know or someone in your area is carrying a gun, report it to the local police on 101.

   - In an emergency dial 999.

   Explain that one strategy that police forces across the UK have been trying is to hold a 'gun amnesty'. This means that for a set amount of time anyone with a gun they don't have a licence

---

18   www.gov.uk/government/publications/serious-violence-strategy

for can hand in their weapon without being prosecuted for possessing a weapon at the point of its surrender. This is unlikely to encourage everyone to come forward, especially anyone using a gun for criminal or violent activity, but it has been deemed successful.

4. In pairs, set the young people the task of going online to research amnesties that have happened over the last two years to find out which have been most successful and why. They should make notes as they go along, as well as writing down which authority they have been looking at to see how success varied in different parts of the country. From here they should select the authority they feel has been most successful in terms of numbers of weapons received and positive feedback, ready to present back to the rest of the group.

Invite each group to share their findings using the following questions to prompt discussion between presentations:

–   Do gun amnesties work? How or why?

–   What do you think prevents more weapons being handed in?

–   Do you think that more gun amnesties would encourage more people to surrender theirs? How or why?

WEAPON CRIME

A gun threat on the Twitter feed of a female MP	A threat to shoot a footballer in the legs if he doesn't play better shouted during a match
A photo on Instagram of guns and knives next to a piece of paper with a mobile phone number on it	A comment under an online news report supporting a terrorist gun attack
Instructions on how to convert an air rifle to live ammunition on the dark web	A music video featuring guns and sexual images
Hearing someone at school boasting that they have access to a gun	A YouTube clip of a gang shooting in the US
A live petition on Facebook to make possession of a handgun legal in the UK	A family member who has an old firearm from the war hidden away
A meme of someone holding a gun	Unsubstantiated claims that a local gang uses guns to intimidate non-members

ACTIVITY 50: REDUCING WEAPON CRIME

Aims

- To raise awareness about UK laws in place to protect people from weapon crime.

- To discuss the potential consequences of carrying a weapon.

- To consider what else could be done to encourage young people not to carry weapons.

Time: 2 hours

Key vocabulary

- Serious Violence Strategy (2018)[19]

- Crime

- Weapon

- Law

- Consequences

You will need

- Sets of Crime cards

- Sets of Anti-Weapon Crime Policies

- Poster paper

- Art materials (paint, brushes, pens etc.)

How to do it

1. In groups of three, ask the young people to discuss the gang-related crimes outlined on the Crime cards and then to rank them 1–7, with the most serious being '1' (most impact on victim(s) and/or society) and least serious '7'.

2. Call time and invite each group to share the order they have placed the cards in and why. Point out that 'grave' crimes, for example, rape, murder and aggravated assault, will not go to a youth court because the offence is too serious and it will be tried at Crown Court by a jury.

    Inform the young people that despite what they might think, homicides and gun and knife crime account for just 1 per cent of all recorded UK crime, but their impact on society is huge. Because of this the government has made tackling serious violence a top priority, and in April 2018 they set out a new Serious Violence Strategy backed with £40 million of Home Office funding.

3. Divide the young people into groups of five. Ask each to nominate a leader who, for this exercise, is now the Government Minister for Anti-Weapon Crime. The rest of the group will be government advisors. Together, their task is to debate and agree a policy from those outlined on the Anti-Weapon Crime Policies to tackle youth weapon crime and begin to reduce the numbers of young people carrying knives and guns. There is a blank space for them to come up with their own policy too. The Minister should chair the debate, and if the group cannot reach a consensus, this person holds the deciding vote.

4. Allow up to 45 minutes for debate and a decision to be made, encouraging each 'Ministry' to consider how the strategy might be implemented and why they think it will work.

---

19   www.gov.uk/government/publications/serious-violence-strategy

5. Then being the whole group back together. Ask each 'Ministry' to share their policy and the reasons that they have chosen it using the prompt questions below to spark debate:

   – How will this tackle youth weapon crime?

   – What are the pros and cons of this policy?

   – What needs to happen for this strategy to be successful?

   – How should the policy be implemented to get maximum 'buy in' from young people?

   – What else could be done?

6. Back in the same groups, set the young people the task of designing an anti-weapon poster for younger peers. This should raise awareness about the potential consequences of serious violence and encourage them not to carry weapons. It should also have details of how to report weapon crime and where to go for local advice and support.

   The posters can be presented to the other groups and then displayed to raise awareness of the issues after this project ends.

7. Consider developing this into a wider project where the most effective designs are printed and shared with schools as part of a peer education project.

CRIME

Criminal damage	Intimidation with a knife
Drug dealing	Fighting
Hate crime	Carrying a gun without a license
Blackmail	

ANTI-WEAPON CRIME POLICIES

Policy A: Invest in a secondary school education strategy to teach young people about the impact of carrying a dangerous weapon and strategies to resist peer pressure.

Policy B: Make the consequences for being caught in possession of a weapon tougher so that young people face an automatic sentence of five years in a Young Offender Institution if they are caught.

Policy C: Put the responsibility onto parents and carers of under-18s by making them face a large fine and an automatic Parenting Order if those they have responsibility for are caught in possession of a weapon.

Policy D: Sentence any young person arrested for carrying a weapon to work for a year voluntarily in a hospital with the victims of serious violence so they can see the consequences.

Policy E: Hold weapon amnesties in all areas for weapons to be handed in without consequence. Any young person caught with one after that date should be sent to a Young Offender Institution for two years.

Policy F: Any young person caught in possession of a weapon is to be put on a Weapon Offender List. They would need to check in monthly to the police and be subject to random weapon tests where their home and person could be searched.

Policy G: . . . .

. . . .

. . . .

. . . .

. . . .